Religious Speech, Hatred and LGBT Rights

Nijhoff Law Specials

VOLUME 103

The titles published in this series are listed at *brill.com/nlsp*

Religious Speech, Hatred and LGBT Rights

An International Human Rights Analysis

By

Jeroen Temperman

BRILL
NIJHOFF

LEIDEN | BOSTON

Library of Congress Cataloging-in-Publication Data

Names: Temperman, Jeroen, author.
Title: Religious speech, hatred and LGBT rights : an international human rights analysis / by Jeroen Temperman.
Description: Leiden, The Netherlands : Koninklijke Brill NV, [2021] | Series: Nijhoff law specials, 0924-4549 ; volume 103 | Includes bibliographical references and index. | Summary: "Imagine a religious leader who, during the weekly religious service, explains to the flock that members of the LGBT+ (lesbian, gay, bisexual and transgender, plus other types of sexual orientation or gender identity) community are lesser beings, are sick people who need to be cured, or need to be punished, or some such verbal attack. Or, more subtly, imagine a religious believer publicly questioning equal rights for LGBT people in certain areas of public or private life, like equal marriage rights or equal access to certain service or jobs"– Provided by publisher.
Identifiers: LCCN 2021016342 | ISBN 9789004458857 (paperback) | ISBN 9789004458864 (ebook)
Subjects: LCSH: Sexual minorities--Legal status, laws, etc. | Freedom of religion. | Hate speech–Law and legislation.
Classification: LCC K3242.3.T462021 | DDC 342.08/7–dc23
LC record available at https://lccn.loc.gov/2021016342

Typeface for the Latin, Greek, and Cyrillic scripts: "Brill". See and download: brill.com/brill-typeface.

ISSN 0924-4549
ISBN 978-90-04-45885-7 (paperback)
ISBN 978-90-04-45886-4 (e-book)

This book is printed on acid-free paper and produced in a sustainable manner.

For Irene, Samuel, Jonathan

Contents

Foreword

How to respond to 'hate speech' in a human-rights-compliant manner is not one of the easiest international-law questions. Anyone brave enough to venture into this intellectual minefield will be called upon, sooner or later, to tackle several crucial – often interrelated – issues. Is there a difference between 'unprotected' and 'prohibited' speech? I.e., are states allowed to outlaw some forms of hate speech without being, strictly speaking, required to do so under existing international rules? Which is the behaviour that these rules seek to constrain? For example, should national criminal law opt for 'high-threshold' (incitement to violence or discrimination) or 'low-threshold' (defamation and insult) offences? May one qualify as a potential victim of hate speech without belonging to a group sharing certain characteristics such as those expressly mentioned in the international provisions banning discrimination? Most importantly, is it possible to devise anti-hate-speech rules that do not require, when applied to concrete cases, a balancing exercise between competing rights?

Religious hate-speech – the destructive effects of which are palpable for minorities like the Jewish and the Muslim – raises problems of its own, often related to demands for privileged treatment made by believers. Jeroen Temperman in his latest cutting-edge study addresses – in his usual meticulous way, within the difficult conceptual framework described above – one such demand, which had not received until recently the attention it deserved in legal literature. May one rely on his/her freedom of religion or belief (FORB) to claim the right to engage in what others would qualify as homo/transphobic speech?

This is a real problem (much more taxing than another demand for privileged treatment, known as the defamation-of-religion exception), given the challenge that sexual-orientation and gender-identity questions genuinely present for many faithful. (High-publicity discrimination cases litigated on both sides of the Atlantic, such as *Eweida* and the same-sex-wedding-cake ones, attest to this.) As Temperman shows through extensive comparative research, the question has exercised the legislator and courts of many pluralist democracies. Letting oneself be guided by one's 'liberal' instincts may, of course, lead to some answers. Thus, recognising an absolute 'scripture defence' would seem a rather dubious proposal; as the author points out, this would have struck the balance between FORB and LGBT rights a priori in favour of the former, always sheltering some forms of hate speech from the threat of persecution. Many dilemmas, however, remain. Can one, for example, use the hate-speech argument to question the right of religion to define sin? Or deny to a considerable segment of the population the opportunity to contribute their perspectives to important social debates?

In this book Temperman approaches these complex, emotionally charged issues in a dispassionate manner, methodically 'unpacking' all related questions: how sexual orientation and gender identity came to be recognised as protected characteristics in international anti-discrimination law; how the members of the LGBT+ community became part of the 'others' whose rights have to be balanced against freedom of expression and religion under the European Convention on Human Rights (the ECHR – an interesting situation where 'othering' becomes a legal victory); and how the European Court of Human Rights (the ECtHR) has gradually recognised a duty to prosecute hate speech, aligning the ECHR with the ICCPR (the Covenant) and ICERD. While doing so, he covers an impressive array of international material. He also highlights the differences between forms of hate speech that states *must* forbid under Article 20(2) of the Covenant and forms that states *may* punish under Article 10 of the ECHR.

Temperman's book contains three key propositions, each made with remarkable clarity. First, the practice of states belonging to the Western European and Others Group (WEOG – this being one of the UN 'regions'), seen in the light of consistent treaty bodies' findings, has created a regional custom, prohibiting incitement to violence or discrimination against the LGBT+ community. This is a significant development, as anti-incitement rules form an essential emancipation tool. Secondly, international supervision can help unify the level of protection afforded to the LGBT+ community, in this respect. Laws in the 'regions' surveyed (WEOG and, to a certain extent, Latin America) often have gaps, not covering all potential victims – especially trans people. Statutory reform is, of course, necessary in an area of law where semantics often hide a considerable degree of bias.

Thirdly, once the 'scripture defence' is set aside, one can safely rely on the UN Rabat Plan of Action to create a robust theoretical framework for examining allegations of religious incitement to homo/transphobic violence or discrimination. Temperman proposes, in this connection, a fine contextual analysis based on six parameters, each one of which performs a well-explained function in the balancing of freedom of expression and religion against LGBT rights. He also makes useful suggestions about third-party expert input to the adjudication process and socio-legal research that can help gauge, among other things, the vulnerability of each target group and the likelihood that, in any given situation, it will be impacted by homo/transphobic incitement. This makes fascinating reading, especially when precedent is discussed in a critical manner (*Hammond v. DPP*, which resulted in a conviction for the believer); also when it is shown how better results were obtained in one of the rare – one might stress – cases that did not involve Christian defendants (*R. v. Ilhaz Ali, Razwan Javed and Kabir Ahmed*).

The conclusions reached are not only thoroughly thought-out. They are also highly relevant for the work of many international human-rights monitoring bodies and courts. The ECtHR would be one of them. Anyone vaguely familiar with its case law knows that the 'subsidiarity' approach, currently favoured in Strasbourg, involves setting parameters at the European level that will guide national judges (enjoying a margin of appreciation) in their search for the right equilibrium between competing interests. The parameters to be used in cases of religiously motivated homo/transphobic speech may well be found in Temperman's latest book.

Admittedly, the author's threshold for punishing such speech is rather high. This should not be taken to indicate bias in favour of believers. It rather reflects a principled position vis-à-vis hate speech in general. Moreover, nothing excludes that a similarly well-structured balancing-exercise can be conducted in respect of the lower-threshold offences tolerated under the ECHR.

Undoubtedly, *Religious Speech, Hatred and LGBT Rights* has much to commend it. One caveat must, of course, be entered. The author does not hide that his proposals mostly concern liberal democracies. However, he does recall that often regional customs gradually evolve into international standards. Moreover, setting the threshold high may be necessary if the aspiration is to create a universal obligation for states to punish homo/transphobic speech. This groundbreaking book, rich in international sources and comparative material, with its outstandingly subtle analysis of highly contested issues, could turn out to be the stepping-stone for the recognition of such an obligation.

Stephanos Stavros
Senior Legal Adviser to the Director General of Human Rights and the Rule of Law, Council of Europe

Acknowledgments

This book greatly benefitted from discussions with many people. Thanks to my colleagues at the Department of International and European Union Law at Erasmus School of Law, who commented on early versions of this work. Thanks to Roland Pierik for the invitation to present an early version of this book at a colloquium organised by the Paul Scholten Centre of Jurisprudence at the University of Amsterdam Law School and thanks to all his colleagues for their valuable feed-back. Many thanks to Hannah Driesens for her help in finalizing the tables of (case) law. Special thanks go to the following persons, who have been extremely generous with their time and who have provided me with detailed comments on draft versions of the manuscript: Wibren van der Burg, Richard Moon, Marloes van Noorloos, Stephanos Stavros and Stephanie Triefus.

JT
Rotterdam, February 2021

Table of International Law

Treaties / Binding Instruments

Soft Law

Table of National Law

Table of International Cases

Table of National Cases

BRAZIL

Supreme Court of Brazil, Judgement of 13 June 2019 [*sexual orientation*], 39

CANADA

Hellquist v. Owens, [2002] 228 SASK. R. 148, 2 (Sask. Q.B.), 63

Lund v. Boissoin, 2012 ABCA 300 (CanLII), 65

Owens v. Saskatchewan (Human Rights Commission), 2002 SKQB 506 (CanLII), 63

Owens v. Saskatchewan (Human Rights Commission), 2006 SKCA 41, 63-64

Saskatchewan (Human Rights Commission) v. Bell, [1994] 21 C.R.R. (2d) 92, 30 (Sask. App. Ct.), 63

Saskatchewan (Human Rights Commission) v. Whatcott, 2013 SCC 11, [2013] 1 S.C.R. 467, 62-63

FRANCE

Cour de Cassation, *Christian X*, Case No. 07-83398, judgment of 12 November 2008, 75

MEXICO

Mexican Supreme Court, Judgment of 6 March 2013 [*homophobic slurs*], 38

NETHERLANDS

'*Donkey trial*' (1966–1968), 2

High Court of The Hague, *el-Moumni*, Case No. 2200359302, Judgment of 18 November 2002, 58

Court of Rotterdam, *el-Moumni*, Case No. 10/040070-01, Judgment of 8 April 2002, 59

Gerechtshof Amsterdam, *Felter*, Case No. 23-004790-14, Judgment of 1 February 2016, 76-77

Hoge Raad, *Felter*, Case No. 13/01327, Judgment of 16 December 2014, 76

Hoge Raad, *Ismo*, Case No. 17/01485, Judgment of 26 June 2018, 76

Hoge Raad, *Van Dijke*, Case No. 00945/99, Judgment of 9 January 2001, 59

Court of Amsterdam, Case No. 13/659330-16, Judgment of 4 January 2019, 85

High Court of Arnhem, Case No. 21-000117-00, Judgment of 26 June 2001, 59

NEW ZEALAND

Court of Appeal of New Zealand, *Living Word Distributors Ltd v. Human Rights Action Group (Wellington)*, 37

SOUTH AFRICA

High Court of South Africa (Western Cape Division, Cape Town), *South African Human Rights Commission v. Oscar Peter Bougaardt*, Case No. EC13/2013, Judgment of 18 May 2018, 66, 75

SWEDEN

Supreme Court of Sweden, *Prosecutor General v. Åke Green*, Case No. B1050-05, Judgment of 29 November 2005, 58, 60, 61

TURKEY

Constitutional Court of Turkey, *Sinem Hun*, Case No. 2013/5356, Judgment of 8 May 2014, 48

UNITED KINGDOM

Birmingham County Court, *Anthony Rollins v. West Midlands Police*, decision of 10 December 2010, 84-85

Court of Appeal, *R. (Ngole) v. University of Sheffield*, [2019] EWCA Civ 1127, Judgment of 3 July 2019, 75

Derby Crown Court, *R. v. Ihjaz Ali, Razwan Javed and Kabir Ahmed*, judgments of 20 January 2012 and 10 February 2012, 83, 86

Divisional Court, *Hammond v. DPP*, [2004] EWHC 69 (Admin), xi, 62, 77-78, 83, 85,

R. (Miller) v. The College of Policing & The Chief Constable of Humberside, [2020] EWHC 225 (Admin), Judgment of 14 February 2019, 49, 79, 81

UNITED STATES OF AMERICA

2nd District Court of Appeal of Los Angeles, Judgment of 17 March 2010 [*online anti-gay bullying*], 38

Supreme Court, *Obergefell v. Hodges*, 576 U.S. 644 (2015), 4

Supreme Court, *Snyder v. Phelps*, 562 U.S. 443 (2011), 38,

CHAPTER 1

Introduction

1 Introduction

Imagine a religious leader who, during the weekly religious service, explains to the flock that members of the LGBT+ (lesbian, gay, bisexual and transgender, plus other types of sexual orientation or gender identity)[1] community are lesser beings, are sick people who need to be cured, or need to be punished, or some such verbal attack. Or, more subtly, imagine a religious believer publicly questioning equal rights for LGBT people in certain areas of public or private life, like equal marriage rights or equal access to certain services or jobs.

In pluralist societies that value both religious freedom and non-discrimination on grounds of sexual orientation and gender identity, such scenarios pose pertinent questions of human rights law and the dynamics of potentially conflicting rights. Legislators and judiciaries in pluralist countries are increasingly faced with these issues, including for instance the question of whether such religious exposés amount to protected religious speech or if the state, conversely, should step in, curtail such speech in one way or another, perhaps condemn and punish the person behind the speech or publication in the interest of protecting the rights of the verbally attacked group; but if so, when exactly, how, and under what circumstances?

2 Speech Conflicts

There are several speech conflicts imaginable and actually occurring between religious practitioners and LGBT people. 'Speech conflicts' are controversies or disputes between two groups caused by the use of speech,[2] raising the legal

1 From here on, whenever 'LGBT' or 'sexual orientation and gender identity' is used, the whole spectrum of minority or vulnerable sexual orientations and gender identities is referred to, unless it is clear from the context that a specific sexual orientation or gender identity is being focused upon.

2 A dissimilar speech conflict may involve speech acts by LGBT people. While not necessarily expressly aimed against religious practitioners, LGBT speech acts – ranging from collective Gay Pride marches, to individuals simply openly showing their sexual orientation, including through non-verbal expressions like public signs of affection for instance through hand-holding or kissing – could offend religious sensitivities. One interesting domestic example

 DOI:10.1163/9789004458864_002

question as to whether certain speech acts may undermine the rights of the targeted group and hence the question if and when the state may legitimately restrict the freedom of expression. 'Speech act' shall be used throughout this book to denote all forms and modalities of expressing opinions, whether in writing or orally expressed, whether verbally expressed or non-verbally, and whether published or otherwise publicly conveyed or disseminated to others.

Contemporary legal controversies in the present regard concentrate chiefly – for the right or wrong reasons[3] – on the permissible content of speech; that is, whether certain speech acts ought to be protected ('protected speech') or rather restricted or otherwise addressed and tackled ('unprotected speech') or even actively combated by states ('prohibited speech'). This issue is further complicated by potentially conflicting human rights standards: the right to freedom of expression and the right to freedom of religion or belief on the one hand and, on the other, such norms as equality standards, the right to physical integrity, the right to life, while the matter is yet further complicated by specific special prohibitions enshrined in international law urging or obliging states to combat speech acts that qualify as hateful incitement.

The prime controversy focused upon in this book concerns religiously-motivated speech against LGBT people, including outright homophobic speech, but also including more subtle religion-based arguments against, for

---

is the Dutch 'donkey trial' (1966–1968) against gay writer Gerard Reve. Reve's *Nader Tot U* contains a scene in which the writer has sexual intercourse with God incarnated as a donkey. He was prosecuted over charges of blasphemy but ultimately acquitted. Controversially, in recent years some states, including Russia and (at municipal level) Moldova, have adopted measures restricting 'gay propaganda' – so-called propaganda of 'non-traditional' relationships – in the interest of protecting traditional religio-cultural values and morals. Similar laws were considered but ultimately rejected by Ukraine. These conflicts between LGBT emancipation and religious and other sensitivities are beyond the scope of this book. See, e.g., Justine De Kerf, 'Anti-Gay Propaganda Laws: Time for the European Court of Human Rights to Overcome Her Fear of Commitment', 4:1 *DiGeSt: Journal of Diversity and Gender Studies* (2017), pp. 35–48; Caroline H. Voyles and Mariana Chilton, 'Respect, Protect, and Fulfill or Reject, Neglect, and Regress? Children's Rights in the Time of the Russian "Gay Propaganda Law"', 21:2 *Health and Human Rights Journal* (2019), pp. 325–330.

3 In the book's concluding section, an important complementary part to the present fairly binary debate on permitted versus prohibited speech is highlighted. As long as state obligations in the area of international anti-incitement law are not fully crystallized, it is perhaps logical that any and all discussion (including the present book) is chiefly preoccupied with sifting through extremes and identifying benchmarks that help demarcate protected speech and prohibited speech. From the perspective of effective human rights promotion and human rights abuse *prevention*, the concomitant focus on positive measures, including in the area of education, promotion of tolerance, measures involving the media, measures involving religious and political leaders, and so forth, are just as crucial, if not more so.

instance, accruing full equality-before-the-law status to LGBT people. The book's motivating questions, accordingly, include these: When are such speech acts to be safeguarded as religious manifestations and protected religious speech? And when does the protection of the rights of LGBT people allow for justifiable restrictions on such speech? The latter issue includes the important specific sub-question as to whether there are types of anti-LGBT speech that states *must* prohibit, i.e. compulsorily, pursuant international anti-incitement standards.

3 Theoretical Framework

By way of theoretical points of departure, this book's discussions operate within the following theoretical and normative framework. Calibration of potentially colliding fundamental rights, including freedom of speech, religious freedom, protection against hateful incitement, protection of dignity rights, equal treatment, among other relevant norms and international and constitutional standards of protection, is a meaningful legal exercise only within liberal democracies. Plain and simply put, the current discussion is one of *pluralism*. Illiberal and repressive states (or rather their ruling elites) that are adamantly opposed to diversity fall outside that scope. States that do not at least nominally pledge to guarantee universal freedom of religion or belief vis-à-vis adherents of all religious and non-religious beliefs, free speech, equality standards including equality on grounds of sexual orientation and gender identity, protection of the life, security and dignity of all people including of the LGBT+ community, have no interest in calibration of pluralist dilemmas for they reject and actively fight pluralism. States zealously protecting religious homogeneity and nationalisms and states actively prosecuting homosexuality or tolerating societal persecutions of persons based on the latter's sexual orientation or gender identity do not recognize the pluralist dilemmas that form the focus of this book.

Yet, focusing on liberal democracies does not imply that calibrating the rights and interests at stake is a straightforward legal matter. First, while free speech and religious freedom within the free world certainly have a strong and extensive legacy, LGBT+ emancipation is all things considered only in its infancy. Homosexual conduct has been decriminalized mere decades ago. Eradication of discrimination on grounds of sexual orientation in all facets of public and private life is very much a work in project. And legal recognition of same-sex marriages, too, is a gradual process and the tally forms an incomplete patchwork: While the thirty or so such freedom to marriage revolutions, commencing with the Netherlands in 2001, and importantly since 2015 also including the United States,[4] show an important trend, the silence at the international level is deafening. Notably, monitoring bodies like the European Court of Human Rights have not yet joined the momentum. Also, if LGB emancipation is in its infancy, this goes all the more so for emancipation, rights recognition and equal treatment on grounds of gender identity.

In both cases, promotion of sexual orientation rights and promotion of gender identity rights, the international–national law dynamics are complex. That is to say, chiefly the domestic developments run ahead of the international ones, like the example of same-sex marriage recognition made just now indicates. Occasionally, it may be the other way around. The *Rabat Plan of Action*, international benchmarks particularly on advocacy of religious hatred, is a good example and it is anticipated that the gist thereof can be applied by legal analogy to hateful homophobic and transphobic speech, thus forming the normative framework for assessing relevant state practise.

International monitoring bodies may also use domestic trends to actively 'shape' a common position on these matters – something we may see occurring in early international case-law on the basic legal protection rights of homosexuals and transsexuals.[5] These dynamics are not counter-intuitive: International bodies are preoccupied with their legitimacy and their mandates and closely follow domestic trends in state practise so as to time their stepping into ongoing complex fundamental rights debates well; whereas domestic legislators need to be grounded and will firmly gauge societal sentiments before tabling bills on inevitably contentious issues of pluralism involving potentially colliding rights.

All these dynamics, then, can be anticipated too within our present discussion on free religious speech discourse and protection of the LGBT+ community against hateful incitement. Notably, despite widespread hate crimes against LGBT people and the phenomenon of homophobia and transphobia and anti-LGBT hateful incitement, contemporary positive international law may strike as far from crystallized on the question as to where to draw the line between protected and unprotected speech that targets LGBT people. Domestic practise, grounded in said societal momentum, often-times may be

4 Supreme Court, *Obergefell v. Hodges*, 576 U.S. 644 (2015).

5 On this form of 'judicial activism', see Jeroen Temperman, 'Religious Symbols in the Public School Classroom', in Jeroen Temperman (ed.), *The Lautsi Papers: Multidisciplinary Reflections on Religious Symbols in the Public School Classroom* (Leiden/Boston: Brill/Martinus Nijhoff Publishers, 2012), pp. 143–176, at pp. 170–171; and, more generally, 'Are State Churches Contrary to International Law?', 2:1 *Oxford Journal of Law and Religion* (2013), pp. 119–149, at pp. 121–122.

expected to set the tone here, with international monitoring bodies (typically in lieu of international law-making in this area), then, timing interventions on their own part. The latter may range from acknowledging trends, endorsing trends (or, in theory, rejecting them), spurring on trends, to 'taking over', that is, establishing best practice and authoritatively prescribing this as the future way forward. Seeing as domestic developments are indeed very much synergizing with societal sentiments, we can only expect 'trends', 'developments', 'momentum'. Two necessary caveats here are that, again, whenever reference to momentum is made we should not forget the very much confined scope of this book: liberal democracies. Second, as the topic of this book is very much in flux, as we are right in the middle of the trends observed, typically the general directions of these developments can be charted at best. The relatively late emergence of (debate as to) protection for LGBT people, as compared to similar protection based on other grounds (notably religion and ethnicity), against hateful incitement must be understood within the said socio-historical considerations on the gradual legal and societal emancipation of LGBT people over the last decades – and in only parts of the world, at that. While this emancipatory development is a sine qua non – hence the exclusion of repressive states – for this additional protection to emerge, the generic fight against LGBT discrimination may become a cause that is inextricable from the fight against hateful incitement.[6] Put differently, perhaps anti-incitement is increasingly understood as one of the capstones of LGBT emancipation.

What with state practice importantly setting the tone, ahead or at the very least alongside international developments, there is the theoretical risk of fragmentation of anti-incitement law. Scope, guarantees, protections rendered by the relevant provisions may all be at stake here. One obvious aspect that may be anticipated as being a divisive issue is the very concept of 'incitement' itself. Universal (UN) standards on eradicating extreme speech, notably the one enshrined in the International Covenant on Civil and Political Rights,[7] deploy this notion. Not 'hate speech' is to be eradicated under the ICCPR, but 'incitement'. Incitement is a qualified legal term and requires, for the speech act to

6 E.g. *Report of the Special Rapporteur on the promotion and protection of the right to freedom of opinion and expression, Frank La Rue* [*Mission to Italy*], A/HRC/26/30/Add.3 (2014), paras. 66 and 88, suggesting the two go hand in hand.

7 United Nations International Covenant on Civil and Political Rights, G.A. Res. 2200A (XXI), 21 U.N. GAOR Supp. (No. 16) at 52, U.N. Doc. A/6316 (1966), 999 U.N.T.S. 171, entered into force 23 March 1976 ('ICCPR' or 'the Covenant'), Article 20(2). See also International Convention on the Elimination of All Forms of Racial Discrimination, G.A. Res. 2106 (XX), Annex, 20 U.N. GAOR Supp. (No. 14) at 47, U.N. Doc. A/6014 (1966), 660 U.N.T.S. 195, entered into force 4 January 1969 ('ICERD'), Article 4.

become within its ambit, not only to be merely hateful but also actively appealing to specific harmful reactions like *violence* or *discrimination*. Not all forms of 'hate speech', hence, amount to hateful incitement. Also, hateful *incitement* unlike hate speech is interpreted as a *triangular offence*, revolving around an inciter, an audience and a target group, thus revolving around especially complex dynamics involving three different relationships (inciter-audience; inciter-target group; and audience-target group).[8]

As some of the other human rights regimes, notably the regional European Convention on Human Rights, do not contain explicit anti-incitement standards, dissimilar (lower) thresholds for interfering with extreme speech may be sanctioned so as to eradicate what under these regimes would be more generically called 'hate speech' (i.e. speech expressing hatred of a person or group of persons based on one the latter's characteristics, like religion or ethnicity or sexual orientation, but not necessarily including a call for discrimination or violence against the latter). In that light, pioneering state practice may be expected to be informed by both anti-incitement as well as wider anti-hate speech approaches. While 'anti-incitement' is the only correct nomenclature when dealing with the universal instruments,[9] both 'incitement' and 'hate speech' are used in relation to legal and judicial developments in the present area, as much as possible doing justice to the context of the legal regime under consideration.

4 Approach and Outline

This book ventures into this issue by way of charting and explaining what positive international law, authoritative interpretation by international monitoring bodies, and the scholarly legal doctrine, provide in the area of hateful incitement against LGBT people and questions of calibrating free speech and religious freedom with the former (emerging) cause. Furthermore, critically analysing that same body of legal data the ambition of this book is to complement the international legal approach to the present issue with a comprehensive comparative legal analysis of state practice, with a view towards furthering our insights as to best – and bad – practices in this area.

8 Jeroen Temperman, *Religious Hatred and International Law: The Prohibition of Incitement to Violence or Discrimination* (Cambridge: Cambridge University Press, 2016), Chapter 7.3 ('The triangle of incitement').

9 *Ibid.*, pp. 180–186, elaborating the *actus reus* of incitement and distinguishing this from hate speech.

The first matter to be scrutinized in this regard is whether – regardless of the religious or non-religious motive behind the speech act – the protection of LGBT rights may function as a limit on free speech and if so, under what circumstances or judged by what criteria (Chapter 2). While an affirmative answer seems rather intuitive, the question operates against a particular historical legal background: the foundational international human rights documents did not expressly codify LGBT rights.

The next strand of investigation is guided by the question of precisely how pro-active states ought to be in combating anti-LGBT speech (Chapter 3). Here the sub-questions include (i) whether anti-LGBT incitement standards can be distilled from or 'read into' positive international law; and (ii) the related question whether emerging state practice defined by increasing numbers of domestic laws expressly protecting against such forms of hateful incitement are, if not directly mandated, at least compatible with international human rights law. The pertinence of that latter exercise is to establish whether domestic practice is not only more sophisticated than relevant international benchmarks, but also especially to figure out if and to what extent (regional) custom to combat anti-LGBT incitement is shaping up in lieu of more crystallized international guidance on this matter.

Once the position of international and domestic law vis-à-vis anti-LGBT incitement is ascertained, the question of the precise scope of anti-incitement measures arises (Chapter 4). As international law and monitoring bodies' guidance in this area is scant, some general observations based on a review of state practice will be offered by way of an initial orientation on these matters.

Subsequently, our final investigation shifts to a number of concrete case studies, drawn largely from domestic case law, wherein the motive behind the speech act that targets LGBT people is an expressly religious one (Chapter 5). How to balance what amounts to a specific clash of rights, namely the one between free religious speech versus LGBT rights? This latter part of the book, hence, illustrates the lessons learnt from international and comparative law by applying those lessons to a number of concrete cases,[10] i.e. by reviewing domestic case law in light of the recent legal developments in the area of anti-incitement.

---

10 It should be noted at the outset that this is not always a 'fair' assessment in that the present assessment is carried out with the benefit of hindsight, i.e. based on recent advances in our understanding of (international) incitement prohibitions and their legal ramifications, which in turn have been significantly triggered by recent concomitant societal advances. Some of the cases engaged with predate recent (international) benchmarking and conceptualization efforts in the area of incitement and similar efforts within legal scholarship. The objective here is not so much to second-guess those domestic decisions, but to illustrate how emerging benchmarks on incitement may play out in real-life cases and foster insights as to what balanced decisions in this area may look like.

CHAPTER 2

LGBT Rights as 'Rights of Others' in Extreme Speech Cases

1 Introduction

Considering the fact that homosexuals were among the victims of the Nazi repression, the immediate post-World War II human rights movement cannot be said to have been generous to LGBT people. The Universal Declaration of Human Rights and other parts of the International Bill of Rights, like the UN International Covenant on Civil and Political Rights, have omitted any mention of the plight of homosexuals and the need to protect their equality and dignity rights. While contemporary human rights documents have remedied that historical omission and typically at the very least insert 'sexual orientation' into the list of prohibited grounds for making distinctions between persons,[1] those foundational human rights instruments of the 1940s, 1950s and 1960s (and later ones) could only be updated through interpretative techniques by monitoring bodies. As a result, LGBT rights tend to have become mainstreamed with such rights as the right to private and family life as well as the generic equality clauses.

It is in that particular light that the question as to whether LGBT rights may serve as a restriction on free speech becomes a meaningful one: After all, the international human rights instruments – at least the foundational ones – typically did not codify LGBT rights.

2 Sex and Sexual Orientation

It is against that backdrop of codified silence, then, that we now turn to international jurisprudence. In the present specialized context of free (religious) speech and the rights of LGBT people, international case law is scarce. Starting at the universal level of the United Nations, rather than accepting sexual orientation rights as 'rights of others', the UN Human Rights Committee

1 E.g. the 2000 Charter of Fundamental Rights of the European Union includes 'sexual orientation' in its non-discrimination clause (Article 20).

 | DOI:10.1163/9789004458864_003

initially directly subsumed sexual orientation matters under the International Covenant on Civil and Political Rights' reference to 'sex',[2] i.e. under the non-discrimination clauses of the Covenant.[3] A (pragmatic) solution, yet as Committee member Bertil Wennergren observed,[4] there still is additional merit in accepting sexual orientation-based rights as 'rights of others' under substantive human rights clauses since not all relevant LGBT rights claims are necessarily properly addressed in the light of the ground of 'sex' as part of an equal rights assessment. This is precisely what the Committee would do a decade later in a case concerning a discriminatory pension scheme whereby spouses and heterosexual partners could be granted pension benefits as 'partner', but homosexual partners were barred from the same.[5] This time round instead of going down the semantic route, the Committee is steadfast and posits that 'the prohibition against discrimination under article 26 comprises also discrimination based on sexual orientation'.[6] This is now established jurisprudence.[7]

3 'Rights of Others' in the ECHR Context

The question as to whether the freedom of expression may be limited by a state in the interest of protecting LGBT rights has been answered affirmatively most unequivocally at the regional level, namely by the European Court of Human Rights[8] in a case that pretty much revolved around that very issue. In *Vejdeland*

2 United Nations International Covenant on Civil and Political Rights, G.A. Res. 2200A (XXI), 21 U.N. GAOR Supp. (No. 16) at 52, U.N. Doc. A/6316 (1966), 999 U.N.T.S. 171, entered into force 23 March 1976 ('ICCPR' or 'the Covenant').

3 Human Rights Committee, *Toonen v. Australia*, Communication No. 488/1992, UN Doc. CCPR/C/50/D/488/1992, Views of 31 March 1994, para. 8.7. This was in response to the State Party's express query to the Committee through which it sought 'guidance as to whether sexual orientation may be subsumed under the term "… or other status" in article 26' (*ibid.*, para. 6.9).

4 See Individual opinion by Mr. Bertil Wennergren.

5 Human Rights Committee, *Edward Young v. Australia*, Communication No. 941/2000, U.N. Doc. CCPR/C/78/D/941/2000, Views of 6 August 2003.

6 *Ibid.*, para. 10.4.

7 At the dismay of some dissenting Committee members. See the separate (dissenting) opining by Abdelfattah Amor and Ahmed Tawfik Khalil appended to the views in Human Rights Committee, *X. v. Colombia*, Communication No. 1361/2005, UN Doc. CCPR/C/89/D/1361/2005, Views of 30 March 2007, which decision indeed consolidates the Committee's approach (notably at para. 7.2: 'the Committee finds that the State party has violated article 26 of the Covenant by denying the author's right to his life partner's pension on the basis of his sexual orientation').

8 Hereinafter also referred to as the 'Strasbourg Court'.

v. Sweden the Strasbourg Court considered whether restrictions imposed on anti-LGBT speech by members of a Swedish neo-fascist organization could be deemed legitimate.[9] The group called *Nationell Ungdom* (National Youth) had distributed some 100 leaflets at a secondary school by way of depositing these in/on the pupils' lockers.

The flyer read as follows:

> Homosexual Propaganda
>
> In the course of a few decades society has swung from rejection of homosexuality and other sexual deviances to embracing this deviant sexual proclivity. Your anti-Swedish teachers know very well that homosexuality has a morally destructive effect on the substance of society and will willingly try to put it forward as something normal and good.
>
> – Tell them that HIV and AIDS appeared early with the homosexuals and that their promiscuous lifestyle was one of the main reasons for this modern-day plague gaining a foothold.
> – Tell them that homosexual lobby organisations are also trying to play down paedophilia, and ask if this sexual deviation should be legalised.[10]

Individual members of *Nationell Ungdom* – four of whom went on to contest this in Strasbourg – were held responsible for disseminating these leaflets and convicted by Swedish courts, as upheld ultimately by the Swedish Supreme Court, for 'agitation against a national or ethnic group' and sentenced to suspended prison sentences and fines.

At the domestic level Swedish Courts amply engaged with the question how far free speech stretches in the event of speech acts critically targeting LGBT people, a discussion that expressly engaged also the European Convention on Human Rights[11] and relevant guidance by the European Court of Human Rights. The Swedish judiciary[12] – correctly, as the *Vejdeland* judgment would

---

9 European Court of Human Rights, *Vejdeland and Others v. Sweden*, Application No. 1813/07, Judgment of 9 February 2012.

10 *Ibid.*, para. 8 (italics used in original; Swedish bracketed keywords omitted).

11 Convention for the Protection of Human Rights and Fundamental Freedoms, ETS No. 5, 213 U.N.T.S. 222, entered into force 3 September 1953 ('ECHR', or 'European Convention').

12 It should be noted, though, that the final verdict by the Swedish Supreme Court entailed a majority judgment with two out of the five judges conversely finding a breach of the applicants' freedom of expression as promoted by Swedish law and Article 10 ECHR.

prove – reasoned that the Strasbourg Court in a case like this would emphasize the *context* (a school, i.e. a 'relatively sheltered environment', involving young impressionable persons) and that the *intentions* behind the speech act also ought to be closely scrutinized (referred to more generally in the terminology of the Supreme Court as the 'purpose' of the leaflets).[13] In the latter regard, the Supreme Court emphasized that the purpose could not reasonably be deemed to have been a permissible contribution to public debate on the issue of homosexuality but rather an impermissible – also in light of the ECHR – 'assault' on the rights of homosexuals.[14]

While these *Nationell Ungdom* members argued in Strasbourg before the European Court of Human Rights, among other things, that disseminating these leaflets was wholly covered by their freedom of expression pursuant Article 10 of the ECHR, the Swedish Government rebutted that the penalties imposed were legitimate and hence amounted to no breach. Following the standard tripartite ECHR limitation technique, the Government more specifically underscored the legality (the interference must be 'prescribed by law'), legitimacy (the interference must serve a 'legitimate aim') and necessity (the interference must be 'necessary in a democratic society') of the penalties imposed.

In that respect, the Government first pointed to the domestic criminal law in place that proscribed 'agitation against a national or ethnic group', substantiating the legality ('prescribed by law') criteria. Second, and critical for our present purposes, the Government argued that 'the interference with the applicants' right to freedom of expression served legitimate aims within the meaning of Article 10 § 2, with particular emphasis on "the protection of the reputation or rights of others", that is, homosexuals as a group'.[15] Regarding the necessity of the interference, the Government conceded that the scenario at hand amounts to a complex case of colliding rights but insisted that the domestic judicial authorities weighed the conflicting interests in a careful manner. The Government here underscores that what was at stake was a targeted group of individuals with 'a common denominator', i.e. their sexual orientation, which ought to be distinguished from other target groups like governments, politicians, or other actors in the public domain who may be required to have a thicker skin in the face of verbal abuse.[16]

13 *Vejdeland and Others v. Sweden*, para. 15.

14 *Ibid.*, para. 15.

15 *Ibid.*, para. 33.

16 *Ibid.*, para. 36.

The European Court of Human Rights largely concurs with Sweden on the various aspects of the tripartite limitation test, demonstrating that hate speech legislation protecting LGBT people may in fact serve as a limit on free speech under the ECHR. The Strasbourg Court more specifically elaborated as follows on the requirements of legality, legitimacy and necessity. The Court, first, accepts that the agitation offence was neatly laid down in Swedish law. Most important to our present purposes, the Strasbourg Court, rather straightforwardly, accepts that the convictions following the Swedish criminal law offence of 'agitation' served a legitimate aim within the meaning of the ECHR, namely 'the protection of the reputation and rights of others'.[17] The Court here definitively posits that LGBT rights may function as 'rights of others', i.e. may serve as a ground for limitation in relation to codified Convention freedoms. This holding is significant since LGBT rights as such are not mentioned by the European Convention.

In the context of the necessity test, the third prong of the standardized ECHR limitation mechanism, the Court bases Convention protection for LGBT people chiefly on the equality clause. Specifically, the Court stresses 'that discrimination based on sexual orientation is as serious as discrimination based on "race, origin or colour" '.[18] The Court, for this part of its considerations, could build on existing jurisprudence, for instance in the area of LGBT discrimination in the army.[19] Like the Swedish Government, applying the necessity test the Strasbourg Court places particular emphasis on the fact that the homophobic flyers were placed in the lockers of and hence 'imposed' on young, impressionable persons.[20] Other relevant factors, in the view of the Strasbourg Court, included the fact that the Swedish judiciary had carefully considered and balanced the applicants' free speech rights with the legitimate aim of restricting free speech in the interest of promoting the rights or reputations of others. The European Court of Human Rights emphasizes, here, the Swedish Courts' finding that the leaflets were 'unnecessarily offensive'.[21] What also mattered, finally, was that the applicants' convictions incurred only minor penalties (fines and suspended prison sentences), no actual prison sentences, even though the Swedish law against agitation would have sanctioned the latter.[22]

---

17 *Ibid.*, para. 49.

18 *Ibid.*, para. 155.

19 E.g. European Court of Human Rights, *Smith and Grady v. United Kingdom*, Application Nos. 33985/96 and 33986/96, 27 September 1999, specifically concerning discrimination against homosexuals in (policies of) the Royal Navy.

20 *Vejdeland and Others v. Sweden*, para. 56.

21 *Ibid.*, para. 57.

22 *Ibid.*, paras. 58-59.

The upshot of these considerations, then, was that the conviction for incitement ('agitation') against LGBT people was permissible under the ECHR and that the freedom of expression of these members of *Nationell Ungdom* was not violated. Put differently, anti-LGBT hate speech is not necessarily protected speech under the ECHR and may under circumstances be restricted.

4 Concluding Remarks

The UN Human Rights Committee has, after various steps in its proceedings, recognized LGBT rights as 'rights of others', thus as a potential limiting factor vis-à-vis other substantive rights. The European Court of Human Rights permits speech restrictions, based on hate speech legislation, aimed at protecting the rights and reputations of LGBT people.

CHAPTER 3

The Emerging Duty to Prohibit Anti-LGBT Speech

1 Introduction

It is one thing to conclude that in a concrete case LGBT rights may justifiably be mobilized as rights of others so as to curtail an actual instance of extreme speech, it is quite another to conclude that human rights law sanctions a priori speech restrictions in the area of hate speech or hateful incitement. Still another important distinction, should the latter treaty basis for hateful incitement legislation indeed be established, is the one between human rights law *permitting* special limits on freedom of expression with a view towards protecting persons against hatred or hateful incitement, versus international human rights law *obliging* state parties to adopt laws containing such extreme speech restrictions. The objective of this chapter is to pinpoint the state of play under two international human rights regimes, one regional one – that of the European Convention on Human Rights – and one universal, namely that of the United Nations International Covenant on Civil and Political Rights.

A major paradox, which will be gradually unravelled in this chapter, is that the international instruments are relatively clear on anti-incitement as a duty, including questions of legal implementation, but are on their face unclear on the exact grounds of punishable incitement; whereas the regional European Convention system is relatively clear on the need to include the grounds of sexual orientation and gender identity into anti-hate speech policies, but this system then again is unclear as to the precise proactive legislative obligations that flow from the Convention in this regard.

2 The Emerging ECHR Duty to Investigate Homophobic Hate Speech

Starting with the regional European Court of Human Rights, this human rights court did initially not go quite so far as to establish a Convention-based state obligation to ban hate speech, certainly not in the landmark case of *Vejdeland*, but also not in early hate speech cases in general, including judgments in related areas like cases of inter-religious or racist hate speech. Perhaps this stood to reason inasmuch as the ECHR does not actually contain any explicit standards or norms, let alone outright prohibitions, on hate speech or more specifically on hateful incitement. In other words, on its face there is no clear

 | DOI:10.1163/9789004458864_004

mandate for the Court to build a proactive body of anti-incitement jurisprudence on.

Thus, in that reading, the dangers of incitement may certainly play a role as part of the regular limitation system under the right to freedom of expression.[1] Yet finding in a concrete case that a state justifiably limited free speech based on the need to counter incitement so as to protect the rights of others is, naturally, different from the position that anti-incitement laws flow from a human rights treaty in the form of a hard and fast state obligation, as is the case under the ICCPR and the United Nations International Convention on the Elimination of All Forms of Racial Discrimination,[2] treaties to which we will repeatedly return in this chapter.

It is against that background that other organs of the Council of Europe, including political ones like the Committee of Ministers, and including expert bodies like the European Commission against Racism and Intolerance (ECRI),

---

1 ECHR, Article 10 reads in full: '1. Everyone has the right to freedom of expression. This right shall include freedom to hold opinions and to receive and impart information and ideas without interference by public authority and regardless of frontiers. This article shall not prevent States from requiring the licensing of broadcasting, television or cinema enterprises. 2. The exercise of these freedoms, since it carries with it duties and responsibilities, may be subject to such formalities, conditions, restrictions or penalties as are prescribed by law and are necessary in a democratic society, in the interests of national security, territorial integrity or public safety, for the prevention of disorder or crime, for the protection of health or morals, for the protection of the reputation or rights of others, for preventing the disclosure of information received in confidence, or for maintaining the authority and impartiality of the judiciary'. The second paragraph, and especially the ground of 'protection of the reputation or rights of others', may be mobilized in the context of anti-incitement measures.

2 International Convention on the Elimination of All Forms of Racial Discrimination, G.A. Res. 2106 (XX), Annex, 20 U.N. GAOR Supp. (No. 14) at 47, U.N. Doc. A/6014 (1966), 660 U.N.T.S. 195, entered into force 4 January 1969 ('ICERD'), Article 4 which provides: 'States Parties condemn all propaganda and all organizations which are based on ideas or theories of superiority of one race or group of persons of one colour or ethnic origin, or which attempt to justify or promote racial hatred and discrimination in any form, and undertake to adopt immediate and positive measures designed to eradicate all incitement to, or acts of, such discrimination and, to this end, with due regard to the principles embodied in the Universal Declaration of Human Rights and the rights expressly set forth in article 5 of this Convention, inter alia: (a) Shall declare an offence punishable by law all dissemination of ideas based on racial superiority or hatred, incitement to racial discrimination, as well as all acts of violence or incitement to such acts against any race or group of persons of another colour or ethnic origin, and also the provision of any assistance to racist activities, including the financing thereof; (b) Shall declare illegal and prohibit organizations, and also organized and all other propaganda activities, which promote and incite racial discrimination, and shall recognize participation in such organizations or activities as an offence punishable by law; (c) Shall not permit public authorities or public institutions, national or local, to promote or incite racial discrimination'.

have gone, certainly in past times, strikingly and significantly further than did the European Court of Human Rights. The former, the Committee of Ministers, has provided in a recommendation that 'Member states [of the Council of Europe] should take appropriate measures to combat all forms of expression, including in the media and on the Internet, which may be reasonably understood as likely to produce the effect of inciting, spreading or promoting hatred or other forms of discrimination against lesbian, gay, bisexual and transgender persons. Such "hate speech" *should be prohibited* and publicly disavowed whenever it occurs'.[3] By contrast, it may be noted, the Parliamentary Assembly of the Council of Europe has called upon states far more modestly to 'condemn hate speech and discriminatory statements and effectively protect LGBT people from such statements while respecting the right to freedom of expression, in accordance with the European Convention on Human Rights and the case law of the European Court of Human Rights'.[4] It is unclear whether any such 'condemning' and 'effectively protecting' may mean prohibiting, banning, penalizing – in short, combatting through criminalization.

As early as 2002, ECRI posited in general terms that

> an effective legal framework against racism and racial discrimination may be adapted to the specific conditions of each country. They could thus be set out in a single special act or laid out in the different areas of national legislation (civil law, administrative law and penal law). These key components might also be included in broader legislation encompassing the fight against racism and racial discrimination. For example, when adopting legal measures against discrimination, member states might prohibit, alongside racial discrimination, other forms of discrimination such as

3 *Recommendation CM/Rec(2010)5 of the Committee of Ministers to member states on measures to combat discrimination on grounds of sexual orientation or gender identity*, adopted by the Committee of Ministers on 31 March 2010 at the 1081st meeting of the Ministers' Deputies, para. 6 (emphasis added). The caveat is added that '[a]ll measures should respect the fundamental right to freedom of expression in accordance with Article 10 of the Convention and the case law of the Court'. Paras. 7-8 of the same Recommendation further detail a number of positive measures member states can take to prevent or tackle anti-LGBT hate speech.

4 Parliamentary Assembly, *Resolution 1728(2010) on Discrimination on the basis of sexual orientation and gender* identity, Adopted by the Assembly on 29 April 2010 (17th Sitting). In *Resolution 1948(2013) on Tackling discrimination on the grounds of sexual orientation and gender identity*, adopted by the Assembly on 27 June 2013 (26th Sitting), the Parliamentary Assembly moved on to recommend a host of positive measures aiming to prevent or address anti-LGBT hatred (para. 9.2).

> those based on gender, *sexual orientation*, disability, political or other opinion, social origin, property, birth or other status.[5]

In 2015, when ECRI developed more extensive policy recommendations on the issue of combating hate speech, this expert body – despite its mandate being defined by the fight against racism – deemed 'gender identity or sexual orientation' to be part and parcel of any sound international law-based approach to (and definition of) hateful incitement.[6] The Explanatory Memorandum annexed to ECRI's *General Policy Recommendation on Combating Hate Speech* proposes the following definition of hate speech:

> Hate speech for the purpose of the Recommendation entails the use of one or more particular forms of expression – namely, the advocacy, promotion or incitement of the denigration, hatred or vilification of a person or group of persons, as well any harassment, insult, negative stereotyping, stigmatization or threat of such person or persons and any justification of all these forms of expression – that is based on a non-exhaustive list of personal characteristics or status that includes "race", colour, language, religion or belief, nationality or national or ethnic origin, as well as descent, age, disability, sex, gender, *gender identity and sexual orientation.*[7]

---

5 ECRI, *Explanatory memorandum to ECRI General Policy Recommendation No. 7 on National legislation to combat racism and racial discrimination*, para. 4 (emphasis added). ECRI, *General Policy Recommendation No. 7 on national legislation to combat racism and racial discrimination*, adopted on 13 December 2002 and revised on 7 December 2017, itself omits sexual orientation in its hate speech provision (Article 18); the explanatory memorandum remedies that oversight.

6 *ECRI General Policy Recommendation No. 15 on Combating Hate Speech*, adopted on 8 December 2015, preamble and Explanatory Memorandum at para. 6 ('gender identity or sexual orientation'). The two preambular references read as follows: 'Considering that hate speech is to be understood for the purpose of the present General Policy Recommendation as the advocacy, promotion or incitement, in any form, of the denigration, hatred or vilification of a person or group of persons, as well as any harassment, insult, negative stereotyping, stigmatization or threat in respect of such a person or group of persons and the justification of all the preceding types of expression, on the ground of "race", colour, descent, national or ethnic origin, age, disability, language, religion or belief, sex, gender, *gender identity, sexual orientation* and other personal characteristics or status' (emphasis added); and: 'Recalling that the work of ECRI focuses on hate speech on the grounds of "race", colour, language, religion, nationality, national or ethnic origin, *gender identity or sexual orientation* ...' (emphasis added). ECRI has a longer history of engaging with anti-LGBT hatred in the context of its country monitoring procedures, as noted in *ECRI General Policy Recommendation No. 15*, para. 31.

7 Explanatory Memorandum, para. 9 (emphasis added).

The inclusive and steadfast nature of these reports and workings on eradicating hateful speech contrasts sharply with the early case law from the European Court of Human Rights on various forms of hate speech. In the earliest cases the Court would typically not move beyond mobilizing the Convention's abuse of rights clause (Article 17)[8] to declare complaints about restrictions on hateful speech manifestly ill-founded and hence inadmissible.[9] In those cases that were decided on the merits, the regular limitation system would be highlighted to underscore that states under circumstances would be permitted to limit extreme speech in the interests of the reputations or rights of others.[10]

Accordingly, that early body of case-law on *permissible restrictions* did not, among other issues, explain:

(i) whether the Convention contains positive obligations to pro-actively combat hate speech; and more specifically whether incitement laws are required under the Convention and if so, what are the investigative obligations in alleged hateful incitement cases as well as the state obligations in terms of punishing inciters;

(ii) what are the rights of the alleged hate speech victims under the Convention, specifically, does an alleged hate speech victim have legal standing under the Convention to bring a case against a state claiming that the state fails to have appropriate anti-incitement

---

8 ECHR, Article 17, which provides: 'Nothing in this Convention may be interpreted as implying for any State, group or person any right to engage in any activity or perform any act aimed at the destruction of any of the rights and freedoms set forth herein or at their limitation to a greater extent than is provided for in the Convention'. A comparable clause, hence, to for instance Article 5, paragraph 1, of the ICCPR: 'Nothing in the present Covenant may be interpreted as implying for any State, group or person any right to engage in any activity or perform any act aimed at the destruction of any of the rights and freedoms recognized herein or at their limitation to a greater extent than is provided for in the present Covenant'. An important difference between the two human rights treaties, hence, is that the ICCPR contains both a sui generis abuse of rights prohibition *and* a more tailored incitement prohibition forcing specific laws to be in place on the latter specific issue.

9 This 'guillotine approach' to tackling extreme speech, and the very inconsistent usage thereof, has been criticized. See Hannes Cannie and Dirk Voorhoof, 'The Abuse Clause and Freedom of Expression in the European Human Rights Convention: An Added Value for Democracy and Human Rights Protection?', 29:1 *Netherlands Quarterly of Human Rights* (2011), pp. 54–83; David Keane, 'Attacking Hate Speech under Article 17 of the European Convention on Human Rights', 25:4 *Netherlands Quarterly of Human Rights* (2007), pp. 641–663.

10 For a comprehensive analysis of religious hatred cases specifically, see Jeroen Temperman, *Religious Hatred and International Law: The Prohibition of Incitement to Violence or Discrimination* (Cambridge: Cambridge University Press, 2016), offering an analysis of virtually all ECHR hate speech and incitement cases up until 2016.

legislation in place or does not adequately enforce existing anti-incitement legislation;

(iii) as far as the merits of such a complaint are concerned, under what circumstances can such omissions be construed as an actual breach of the right to be protected against hateful incitement; and finally,

(iv) seeing as the Convention does not literally enshrine such a right, into which substantive Convention rights should such protection rights be incorporated?

These are complex questions in their own right, but they have been particularly complicated matters in the context of the European Convention system and its lack of an explicit hate speech provision. In recent years the Strasbourg Court has, however, significantly developed its approach in hate speech cases and appears to be catching up with its Council of Europe colleagues.[11] This has been a gradual process. This trend commenced in dissimilar hate speech areas, notably religious and racist hate speech, while the most recent exponents of this body of case law deals directly with LGBT people and their rights of protection against hateful incitement. It is worth narrating some of the relevant cases, including the ones without an LGBT rights angle, in order to grasp this jurisprudential trend and understand the historical itinerary completed by the Strasbourg Court.

In that regard, an important first stepping stone was the case of *Aksu v. Turkey* inasmuch as legal standing in a hate speech case was now accepted by the European Court of Human Rights.[12] The applicant complained that a book, *The Gypsies* [*sic*] *of Turkey*, published by the Turkish Ministry of Culture and a number of dictionaries contained highly prejudicial views on Roma in Turkey, debasing this group, and through associating Roma with criminality and dishonesty among other negative projections, incited discrimination against this minority. While no determination of a substantive human rights violation was ultimately made, and while the Court noted that the books did not target the applicant directly, the case was groundbreaking inasmuch as the Court deemed that the applicant could nevertheless claim to be a victim under Article 8, thus meeting the admissibility requirements on victim status.[13]

11 And with, as we will see in the next section of this chapter, *infra*, its UN counterparts.

12 European Court of Human Rights, *Aksu* v. *Turkey*, Application Nos. 4149/04 and 41029/04, Grand Chamber Judgement of 15 March 2012.

13 *Ibid.*, paras. 46-54.

The Strasbourg Court went a considerable step further in *Karaahmed v. Bulgaria*.[14] In this case the Court found that highly intimidating and aggressive right-wing and anti-Islamic political protests, convened by nationalist party Ataka, at a mosque amounted to a violation of the positive obligations Bulgaria faces to protect the Muslim population against violent acts of hatred. Rejecting the Article 3 (inhuman and degrading treatment) angle to the case, the Court couched these positive obligations on Article 9 which guarantees religious freedom.[15] Specifically, the respondent state had breached its positive obligations under that provision since it had not sufficiently discharged its *duty to investigate* acts of hateful incitement:

> It is of particular significance that no action has been taken in respect of the most provocative gestures made by the demonstrators at the demonstration. No progress has been made in identifying and charging those responsible for piling and setting fire to the worshippers' prayers rugs, even though the individuals concerned can be clearly seen on the video recordings submitted by both parties to the Court. Nor has any action been taken as regards the cutting of a fez (and the threat that the same would happen to the worshippers) ...[16]

Accordingly, as Stavros puts it, '[t]he judgment clearly establishes that the failure to prosecute hate speech can amount to a breach of the Convention'.[17]

With the exception of the latter case, it appears that 'catch-all'[18] Article 8 on private life of the European Convention is swiftly becoming[19] the main

14 European Court of Human Rights, *Karaahmed v. Bulgaria*, Application No. 30587/13, Judgment of 24 February 2015.

15 It is debatable whether this was the wisest nexus with the Convention. See also Lourdes Peroni, 'Karaahmed v. Bulgaria: The (In)Visible Racial and Religious Motivation of Violence', *Strasbourg Observers* (27 March 2015).

16 *Ibid.*, para. 110.

17 Stephanos Stavros, 'A Duty to Prosecute Hate Speech under the European Convention on Human Rights?', *Oxford Human Rights Hub* (9 April 2015).

18 Article 8 of the ECHR reads: '1. Everyone has the right to respect for his private and family life, his home and his correspondence. 2. There shall be no interference by a public authority with the exercise of this right except such as is in accordance with the law and is necessary in a democratic society in the interests of national security, public safety or the economic well-being of the country, for the prevention of disorder or crime, for the protection of health or morals, or for the protection of the rights and freedoms of others'.

19 Put differently, LGBT rights protection, as expanding into the anti-incitement area, is returning to Article 8. This provision, after all, has been the focal point for equal rights protection of LGBT persons since the early European cases on decriminalizing homosexual conduct. See European Court of Human Rights, *Dudgeon v. United Kingdom*,

avenue for mobilizing fundamental rights against hateful incitement.[20] The same holds true for cases on anti-LGBT hatred. Article 8 has been successfully invoked by the state in order to curtail anti-LGBT speech, i.e. to fence off freedom of expression violations that were claimed by inciters. Article 8 has also been successfully invoked by victims of anti-LGBT speech.

Starting with the former, *Lilliendahl v. Iceland* essentially echoes *Vejdeland* but considerably refines the approach to homophobic hate speech in a number of ways.[21] The applicant had made the following comments online in response to a news item concerning a legal proposal to strengthen education on LGBT matters in primary and secondary schools and concerning also how that issue was recently discussed on Icelandic radio:

> We listeners of [Ú.S.] have no interest in any [expletive] explanation of this *kynvilla* [derogatory word for homosexuality, literally 'sexual deviation'] from [Ó.S.Ó.]. This is disgusting. To indoctrinate children with how *kynvillingar* [literally 'sexual deviants'] *eðla sig* ['copulate', primarily used for animals] in bed. [Ó.S.Ó.] can therefore stay at home, rather than intrude upon [Ú.S.]. How disgusting.[22]

After a number of proceedings with differing outcomes, the Icelandic Supreme Court ultimately convicted Lilliendahl of hate speech on the basis of sexual orientation and gender identity.[23] The European Court of Human Rights concludes that this restriction of his speech was justified. In coming to that conclusion, the Strasbourg Court first brings some order to the European Convention and its hitherto diverse approaches to hate speech. The Court reasons that there are various categories of hate speech and that only the most extreme type, viz. the one whereby violence is directly incited, bumps into Article 17,

---

Application No. 7525/76, Judgment of 22 October 1981; and *Norris v. Ireland*, Application No. 10581/83, Judgment of 26 October 1988.

20 For a comprehensive analysis of recent Strasbourg Court cases through which an obligation to prosecute hate speech is carved out (including in other areas than sexual orientation and gender identity), see Stephanos Stavros, 'Criminal Law Responses to Hate Speech: Towards a Systematic Approach in Strasbourg?', in Laurens Lavrysen & Natasa Mavronicola (eds.), *Coercive Human Rights Positive Duties to Mobilise the Criminal Law under the ECHR* (Oxford: Hart Publishing, 2020), pp. 117–138.

21 European Court of Human Rights, *Carl Jóhann Lilliendahl v. Iceland*, Application No. 9297/18, Judgment of 12 May 2020.

22 *Ibid.*, para. 5 (all bracketed explanations added by the ECtHR).

23 Article 233(a) of the General Penal Code of Iceland, which does not literally contain the words 'hate speech', but the drafting history, so the domestic judgment explains, does allude to this legal notion.

the abuse of rights doctrine. Milder forms of hate speech, i.e. speech through which targeted groups are debased but not directly incited against, like the speech act at hand, ought to be assessed on the merits of the free speech complaint under Article 10 of the Convention.[24] The competing interests, the Court agrees with the Icelandic Supreme Court, are freedom of expression on the one hand and 'on the other hand the right of homosexual persons to private life as guaranteed by ... Article 8 of the Convention'.[25] Hence, whereas in *Vejdeland* LGBT rights were still premised on an abstract 'rights of others' notion, the Strasbourg Court is anchoring LGBT rights more firmly into the concrete right of LGBT people to private life. Finally, focussing chiefly on the speech's content – 'serious, severely hurtful and prejudicial' – both Supreme Court and European Court conclude that the conviction and hence the speech restriction were necessary in a democratic society.[26]

In *Beizaras and Levickas v. Lithuania*, the European Court of Human Rights had already elaborated quite extensively on the significance of Article 8 for hate speech cases and explicitly extends the protection under this provision to victims of anti-LGBT hatred.[27] In other words, *Beizaras* does for LGBT persons what *Karaahmed* did for religious minorities: boost protection against hateful incitement to violence and discrimination in the form of accepting legal standing under the Convention in this type of cases, explicating the positive obligations in the fight against hate speech and, finally, through determining actual breaches of the Convention in that very department.

On the applicability of Article 8, the Strasbourg Court considered that

> comments on the first applicant's Facebook page ... affected the applicants' psychological well-being and dignity, thus falling within the sphere of their private life. ... The fact that human dignity as a constitutional value must be protected by the State has also recently been emphasised by the Constitutional Court ... That being so, and finding that the attacks on the applicants had attained the level of seriousness required for Article 8 to come into play, the Court holds that the facts of the case fall within the scope of Article 8 of the Convention.[28]

24 *Lilliendahl v. Iceland*, paras. 24-26.

25 *Lilliendahl v. Iceland*, para. 44.

26 *Lilliendahl v. Iceland*, para. 45-47.

27 European Court of Human Rights, *Beizaras and Levickas v. Lithuania*, Application No. 41288/15, Judgment of 14 January 2020.

28 *Ibid.*, para. 117.

The Facebook comments at stake concerned reactions to the applicants' posting of a photographed kiss announcing their (same-sex) relationship. This picture went viral and the majority of the 800 comments contained abusive language, including numerous messages inciting violence and discrimination, such as calls for the applicants to be burned, shot, gassed, beaten up, their heads smashed, killed by way of driving with cars over their heads, hanged, sent to the gas chambers, sent to the crematorium, or killed in various other ways.[29]

While Lithuania has expanded its domestic extreme speech legislation so as to cover the ground of sexual orientation,[30] the prosecutorial authorities refused to start criminal investigations and all attempts by the applicants and interventions by LGBT civil society organizations to open such investigations stranded in the Lithuanian courts. The Government's position in this case was twofold: first, the applicants essentially provoked these hostile reactions through their 'eccentric behaviour'; and, second, the impugned statements did not reach the threshold required under Lithuanian anti-incitement law.

The Strasbourg Court ripped both arguments apart. The Lithuanian judiciary's allusion to the applicants' 'eccentric behaviour', the former's emphasizing that the applicants had not opted to post their message exclusively to friends or 'like-minded people' 'even though the Facebook social network allowed such a possibility', the judicial reading of their posted kiss as 'an attempt to deliberately tease or shock individuals with different views or to encourage the posting of negative comments', and the unsubstantiated assumption that criminal investigations would constitute a 'waste of time and resources', showed if anything a bigoted bias on the part of the authorities and was also plain evidence of the fact that the applicants' sexual orientation had everything to do with the authorities' refusal to pursue criminal proceedings.[31]

As far as the threshold question was concerned, the Strasbourg Court held that it

> cannot but observe that other comments, even without calling for violence, regarding the Jews … have been treated by the Lithuanian authorities as falling under Article 170 of the Criminal Code. It also considers that the Government have not provided weighty arguments to refute the applicants' view that if comments such as those uttered in their case did

29 *Ibid.*, para. 10.

30 Criminal Code of Lithuania, Article 170.

31 *Beizaras and Levickas v. Lithuania*, para. 23 (proceedings recap) and paras. 119-124 (assessment).

> not amount to inciting not only hatred but even violence on the basis of the applicants' sexual orientation, then it is hard to conceive what statements would ...[32]

The combination of these findings amount to no less than an indictment of Lithuanian's institutionalized homophobia, which is currently causing serious rule of law failures. Determining a violation of Article 14 (equality) in conjunction with Article 8 on private life, the Strasbourg Court

> ... finds it established, firstly, that the hateful comments including undisguised calls for violence by private individuals directed against the applicants and the homosexual community in general were instigated by a bigoted attitude towards that community and, secondly, that the very same discriminatory state of mind was at the core of the failure on the part of the relevant public authorities to discharge their positive obligation to investigate in an effective manner whether those comments regarding the applicants' sexual orientation constituted incitement to hatred and violence, which confirmed that by downgrading the danger of such comments the authorities at least tolerated such comments ... In the light of those findings the Court also considers it established that the applicants suffered discrimination on the grounds of their sexual orientation.[33]

In sum, the judgment further establishes the 'duty to investigate', which first emerged in *Karaahmed*, instances of hateful incitement and extends this duty into the area of anti-LGBT hatred. Moreover, the Court also elaborates further on the wider positive duties, including criminal law protection, in the area of combating hateful anti-LGBT incitement:

> ... criminal sanctions, including against the individuals responsible for the most serious expressions of hatred, inciting others to violence, could be invoked only as an *ultima ratio* measure ... It considers that this equally applies to hate speach [*sic*] against persons' sexual orientation and sexual life. The Court observes that the instant case concerns undisguised calls on [*sic*] attack on the applicants' physical and mental integrity ... *which require protection by the criminal law*'.[34]

---

32 *Ibid.*, para. 125.

33 *Ibid.*, para. 129.

34 *Ibid.*, para. 128 (final italics added). Moreover, in the section of the judgment listing the general principles under the ECHR applicable to hate speech the Court furthermore

A revolutionary judgment in all regards, it significantly aligns, as we will see next, protection against hateful incitement with similar duties under the UN mechanisms. To recap, hate speech in the Strasbourg Court's early case law functioned as an ambiguous notion to deny admissibility to ostensible inciters or the need to combat it could function as a special limit on free speech with a view towards protecting the reputations and rights of others; more recently, hate speech victims have standing to bring complaints under the Convention alleging non-implementation of the positive obligation to tackle hate speech, with Article 8 becoming the main point of reference in that regard. State parties to the European Convention not having inclusive criminal law protection in place to combat hateful incitement against LGBT persons or not properly investigating incidents of hateful incitement against LGBT persons under those laws are liable to be condemned by the Strasbourg Court pursuant the Convention's (equal) right to private life.[35]

3 Inclusive Incitement Prohibitions: The Theory of Mainstreaming LGBT Protection

Let us now delve deeper into the international standards against hateful incitement. International human rights instruments do, in sharp contrast to the European Convention on Human Rights, contain express anti-incitement clauses from which clear-cut legislative obligations flow on eradicating hateful incitement. However, whereas steadfast in terms of their pronounced and obligatory nature, these standards are at least on their face deficient in one important respect: They have conspicuously omitted 'sexual orientation' and 'gender identity' among the prohibited incitement grounds.

Starting with the compulsory nature of these anti-incitement provisions, the UN Committee on the Elimination of Racial Discrimination has since long accepted that Article 4 of ICERD contains an obligation to have anti-incitement legislation in place, and that the provision enshrines protection

repeatedly states that with respect to the most extreme calls for violence criminal law measures are required rather than merely permitted: 'where acts that constitute serious offences are directed against a person's physical or mental integrity, only efficient criminal-law mechanisms can ensure adequate protection and serve as a deterrent factor ... The Court has likewise accepted that criminal-law measures were required with respect to direct verbal assaults and physical threats motivated by discriminatory attitudes' (*ibid.*, para. 111).

35 *I.e.* taking Articles 8 and 14 of the ECHR in conjunction.

rights against hateful incitement, that incitement victims have standing under this provision to bring complaints, and that the Committee is indeed competent to pronounce independent violations of this provision in the face of faulty anti-incitement efforts on the part of the state, be it the absence of appropriate laws prohibiting incitement or the insufficient enforcement thereof.[36]

The UN Human Rights Committee for its part has been more slow-going in this regard. While the terminology of the incitement clause makes it self-evident that the ICCPR, too, requires domestic laws prohibiting incitement, General Comment No. 34 makes an end to any remaining doubts:

> What distinguishes the acts addressed in article 20 from other acts that may be subject to restriction under article 19, paragraph 3 [the general limitation clause under the freedom of expression provision], is that for the acts addressed in article 20, the Covenant indicates the specific response required from the State: their prohibition by law ... It is only with regard to the specific forms of expression indicated in article 20 that States parties *are obliged* to have legal prohibitions.[37]

Furthermore, while in 2009 the Human Rights Committee in a case concerning anti-Roma speech still obstinately refused to determine 'whether article 20 may be invoked' by an alleged victim of hateful incitement,[38] in a 2016 decision concerning The Netherlands it became clear that Article 20(2) of the ICCPR provides standing to persons claiming to be victims of hateful incitement.[39]

---

36 See, e.g., Committee on the Elimination of Racial Discrimination, *L. K. v. The Netherlands*, Communication No. 4/1991, U.N. Doc. A/48/18 at 131, Views of 16 March 1993; Committee on the Elimination of Racial Discrimination, *The Jewish Community of Oslo et al. v. Norway*, Communication No. 30/2003, U.N. Doc. CERD/C/67/D/30/2003, Views of 15 August 2005.

37 Human Rights Committee, *General Comment No. 34: Article 19: Freedoms of Opinion and Expression*, CCPR/C/GC/34 (2011), paras. 51-52 (emphasis added; paragraph numbers omitted).

38 Human Rights Committee, *Maria Vassilari et al. v. Greece*, Communication No. 1570/2007, Views of 19 March 2009, para. 6.5. This was to the dismay of dissenting Committee member Mr. Abdelfattah Amor, joined by Mr. Ahmad Amin Fathalla and Mr. Bouzid Lazhari, stating in a separate opinion (para. 1): 'The Committee has not ventured an opinion on the applicability of article 20, paragraph 2, to individual cases. While it may, of course, decide to do so in the future, the reasons for evading the question are puzzling ... By declining to give an opinion on this aspect of the communication, the Committee allows uncertainty to persist on the scope of article 20, paragraph 2, particularly as, given the points raised, discussion was needed at the very least with regard to the question of admissibility'.

39 Human Rights Committee, *Rabbae, A.B.S. and N.A. v. The Netherlands*, Communication No. 2124/2011, Views adopted on 14 July 2016.

The case revolved around statements made by Dutch politician Geert Wilders about Muslims and Moroccans which, according to the applicants, amounted to the threshold of hateful incitement and which The Netherlands was obliged to prohibit under the Covenant. While the Human Rights Committee did ultimately not condemn The Netherlands as it found that the incitement legislation in place corresponds to Article 20(2) of the ICCPR and was – despite the eventual conclusion not to penalize Mr. Wilders – effectively implemented in the form of genuine investigations and court proceedings, it remains an important case since it was the very first time the Committee judged an incitement case brought by alleged incitement victims on the merits and firmly dismissed the state party's admissibility concerns.[40]

Accordingly, the provision certainly has teeth, yet it lacks width. The International Covenant on Civil and Political Rights is very specific on what kind of extreme speech is to be banned: Article 20(2) ICCPR lists as prohibited incitement grounds merely 'nationality', 'race' and 'religion'. The provision reads in full: 'Any advocacy of national, racial or religious hatred that constitutes incitement to discrimination, hostility or violence shall be prohibited by law'.[41]

The drafters of the ICCPR had the Holocaust fresh in mind when they crafted this and other provisions, and were chiefly thinking of the Nazi propaganda machinery stirring up virulent anti-Semitism. The 'selectivity' of Article 20(2)

40 In the latter regard, the Human Rights Committee 'notes the State party's argument that article 20 of the Covenant is not cast in terms of a justiciable right. However, the Committee considers that in stating that "any advocacy of national, racial or religious hatred that constitutes incitement to discrimination, hostility or violence shall be prohibited by law", article 20(2) provides protection for people as individuals and as members of groups against this type of discrimination. The article is designed to give specific recognition to the prohibition on discrimination set forth in article 26 of the Covenant, by identifying a limitation that States parties must impose on other enforceable Covenant rights, including the principle of freedom of expression under article 19 of the Covenant. The Committee considers that article 20(2) accordingly does not merely impose a formal obligation on States parties to adopt legislation prohibiting such conduct. Such a law would be ineffective without procedures for complaints and appropriate sanctions. The invocation of article 20(2) by individuals who have been wronged accordingly follows the logic of protection that underlies the entire Covenant' (*Rabbae, A.B.S. and N.A. v. The Netherlands*, para. 9.7).

41 The observant reader will notice that in the present book the prescribed result of 'hostility' is largely avoided. Elsewhere it has been argued that insertion of this term into an otherwise highly qualified incitement prohibition is highly problematic. Dismantling this potentially vast and low-threshold (and even tautological) incitement 'result' is best done through defining it on a par with 'violence', i.e. requiring more than a hostile mind-set. See Temperman, *supra* note 3, pp. 186–190.

ICCPR, as ARTICLE 19 (free speech NGO) puts it, 'may be attributed to the political context of the negotiations and the specific historical events [the drafters] were responding to'.[42] That explanation or justification of the limited prohibited incitement grounds – race, religion and nationality – reflected in Article 20(2), however, fails to appreciate the fact that homosexuals were amongst the victims of Nazism too.[43] The *travaux préparatoires* generally ignores the plight of this group and there is no exception to this in the drafting history pertaining to Article 20(2) specifically.

Now, our question is whether or not this omission indeed means that under the ICCPR State parties are obliged to prohibit racist hateful incitement and hateful incitement based on religion and nationality yet not anti-LGBT incitement. There are several readings, it will be argued next here, of the ICCPR possible that bring homophobic and transphobic speech, and other hateful speech based on sexual orientation or gender identity, within the scope of Article 20(2) of the ICCPR.

The first legal stratagem is a semantic one and relates to the term 'religious hatred'. While the term 'religion', it may be contended, is clear (within the context of the Covenant and its freedom of religion clause this notion is construed broadly and inclusively),[44] the combination 'religious hatred' is rather more unusual within international law and hence open to interpretation. On its face, this term may refer to *hatred targeting a religious group* as well as to *any type of religiously-motivated hatred*. Although one may very well contend that it is evident the drafters had the former particularly in mind (protection against racial and religious intimidation and marginalization), it is not at all evident that the second reading ought to be categorically rejected from a treaty-interpretation perspective. The relevance of this complementary reading lies in the fact that religiously-motivated hatred is *not necessarily aimed at a religious group*.

42 ARTICLE 19, *Responding to Hate Speech against LGBTI People: Policy Brief* (2013). See also ARTICLE 19, *Prohibiting Incitement to Discrimination, Hostility or Violence: Policy Brief* (2012), at p. 12.

43 E.g. Richard Plant, *The Pink Triangle: The Nazi War Against Homosexuals* (New York: Henry Holt & Company Inc, 1986).

44 Freedom of religion or belief under Article 18 of the ICCPR 'protects theistic, non-theistic and atheistic beliefs, as well as the right not to profess any religion or belief'. Human Rights Committee, *General Comment No. 22: Article 18*, HRI/GEN/1/Rev.1 at 35 (1994), para. 2. Moreover, the Human Rights Committee has held that '[t]he terms "belief" and "religion" are to be broadly construed. Article 18 is not limited in its application to traditional religions or to religions and beliefs with institutional characteristics or practices analogous to those of traditional religions' (*ibid.*, para. 2).

The distinction between the two categories is somewhat belied by the question of personal motivation. That is, 'hatred aimed at a religious group' is inevitably also religiously motivated, for any type of 'religious hatred' necessarily combines both intrinsic and extrinsic motivations. While one could in the abstract 'hate' (specific characteristics of) a religious group in and for itself, such hatred at the same time points at a minimum degree of intrinsic feelings of superiority. As this intrinsic motivation can be premised on any belief the inciter holds, including the absence of religious beliefs, it will become clear that religious hatred without a particular, personalized religious motive is bordering on the impossible.

Be that as it may, those considerations hardly serve to reject the reading of 'religious hatred' as religiously-motivated hatred but if anything strengthen that analysis. The fact remains, after all, that the Covenant does not single out 'religious groups' for protection, but is premised on a need to eradicate (inciteful) 'religious hatred', thus leaving open the question of the exact nexus between the qualification of 'religious' and *inciter* (and its potentially religious motivation) and/or *incitee* (and its religious characteristics). This notion of open-endedness of 'religious hatred' does resonate with the Human Rights Committee's approach. Admittedly, the Committee is generally preoccupied with the question whether the targeted group is a religious one, but also the motivations of the inciter are deemed relevant in cases of alleged religious hatred. Thus, in a case concerning the conviction of an anti-Semitic school teacher both the nature of the targeted group was mentioned in direct nexus with the notion of religious hatred ('Jewish communities' right to be protected from religious hatred') as well as the teacher's personal religious motivations (he had 'called upon true Christians to not merely question the validity of Jewish beliefs and teachings but to hold those of the Jewish faith and ancestry in contempt').[45] Accordingly, both the inciter's religious motivations and the target group's religious characteristics have been highlighted and hence deemed to be pertinent in the context of jurisprudential applications of Article 20(2) ICCPR and its key term 'religious hatred'.

The present interpretative stratagem, aiming at the conceptualization of religiously-motivated hatred, has as clear strength that it serves to bring incitement against LGBT people (and other potential target groups, notably women) into the ambit of Article 20(2) ICCPR. This argumentation also has a clear weakness and a clear downside, though. A major weakness is that cases

45 Human Rights Committee, *Malcolm Ross v. Canada*, Communication No. 736/1997, CCPR/C/70/D/736/1997 (2000), Views of 18 October 2000, para. 11.5.

like *Ross* have not definitively shown that the Human Rights Committee would apply the notion of 'protection from religious hatred' in the event the facts of a case were to solely point to religious motivations on the part of the inciter but not at the same time to ostensible religious characteristics on the part of the targeted group. The proof of the pudding would be a case of religiously-motivated incitement against LGBT people, but no such case has been dealt with by the Committee yet as far as the individual communication (complaint) procedure is concerned.[46] In other words, there is in the Committee's jurisprudence as yet no answer to be found to the question whether 'religious' must be cumulatively brought into connection with both inciter and incitee (i.e. and/and) or whether Article 20(2) is engaged also if only one of the two connections can be definitively made (i.e. either/or).

Moreover, a major downside of the above legal stratagem of bringing LGBT people into the scope of Article 20(2) is as follows: Yes, hatred of LGBT people may thus come into the ambit of the incitement clause, but *only if and to the extent* that this hatred is expressly religiously motivated. Accordingly, under the ICCPR, then, there would be no remedy for incitement against sexual orientation minorities which is not (necessarily) religiously motivated, for instance, incitement to violence against LGBT people by neo-Nazis,[47] Alt-Right groups[48] or other (nominally) secular homophobic groups or movements. This would hence lead to the unsatisfactory situation wherein some forms of hatred are more or less immunized due to the motivations on which the inciter premised its hatred. Moreover, the rather ironic upshot of the current stratagem may even be that religious speech is scrutinized more strictly than fascist speech while the Covenant was, among other reasons, crafted to better protect religionists and to make life of fascists more difficult.

This brings us to a second stratagem, which posits that the characteristics mentioned by Article 20(2) are not exhaustive. One could read Article 20(2) on incitement in conjunction with Articles 2 and 26 of the ICCPR on equality and by mainstreaming the suspect grounds mentioned in the latter provisions expand the scope of the former. While this does not immediately bring

46 See *infra* in this chapter, however, for relevant considerations made by the same Committee in the context of the state reporting procedure.

47 *E.g.* European Court of Human Rights, *Vejdeland and Others v. Sweden*, Application No. 1813/07, Judgment of 9 February 2012, revolving around homophobic speech by neo-Nazis.

48 *E.g.* the youth wing of the Dutch Alt-Right political party Forum voor Democatie was exposed by a Dutch newspaper in November 2020 in this regard. Screenshots of the movement's app-group revealed virulent and inciting anti-Semitic as well as homophobic messages. Harm Ede Botje en Mischa Cohen, 'Nazifoto's geen bezwaar bij de jongeren van Forum voor Democratie', *Parool*, 21 November 2020.

'sexual orientation' into play, since this ground is (unlike 'sex') not expressly mentioned in this – 1960s and hence pre-emancipation of LGBT people – document, the relevance of such a mainstreaming exercise lies in the fact that the ICCPR's equality clauses *are* indisputably non-exhaustive ('or other status')[49] and, in any event, the UN Human Rights Committee has expressly remedied the omission of 'sexual orientation' through its equality clause-oriented jurisprudence.[50] Accordingly, this reading brings the protection ground of sexual orientation directly within the ambit of Article 20(2).

It should be noted, however, that ICCPR commentators like Nowak have taken the opposite view and contend that the prohibited grounds mentioned by Article 20(2) are in fact exhaustive and that as a consequence other forms of incitement, like inciting violence against women,[51] but presumably also in his view anti-LGBT incitement, would not fall under Article 20(2)'s prohibition.[52] Nowak does not comment on the question whether this would be any different if the incitement to violence would be religiously motivated.

Whether the words 'national, racial or religious' were intended by the drafters to be exhaustive or not, it is clear in any event that from a contemporary human rights perspective they strike as overly limited.[53] There are contemporary forms of incitement – notably on grounds of sexual orientation and gender identity, but think also of incitement to violence against women, incitement against persons with a disability, among other non-listed grounds – that are just as atrocious, repugnant and objectionable as incitement based on the three grounds expressly recognized by the Covenant. This is also what

---

49 This open-ended phrase 'or other status' can be found both in Article 2 and Article 26 of the ICCPR.

50 Human Rights Committee, *Toonen v. Australia*, Communication No. 488/1992, un Doc. CCPR/C/50/D/488/1992, Views of 31 March 1994; Human Rights Committee, *Edward Young v. Australia*, Communication No. 941/2000, U.N. Doc. CCPR/C/78/D/941/2000, Views of 6 August 2003.

51 Manfred Nowak, *U.N. Covenant on Civil and Political Rights: CCPR Commentary* (2nd rev. edn., Kehl: N.P. Engel Publishers, 2005), at pp. 474–475.

52 For another (dissimilar to Nowak's) opposite view, see e.g. Eric Heinze, 'Cumulative Jurisprudence and Human Rights: The Example of Sexual Minorities and Hate Speech', in Phil C.W. Chan (ed.), *Protection of Sexual Minorities since Stonewall: Progress and Stalemate in Developed and Developing Countries* (London/New York: Routledge, 2010), pp. 62–78. It should be noted, however, that Heinze is against any incitement legislation, his argument against anti-gay hate speech legislation largely being an extension of that position.

53 See also ARTICLE 19, *Responding to Hate Speech against LGBTI People: Policy Brief* (2013) at p. 12, p. 21 and p. 25, making a comprehensive case for applying the 'living instrument' approach to Article 20(2) of the ICCPR necessitating reading 'sexual orientation' into this provision.

the human rights NGO Interrights contends (through its intervention as third-party intervener in the case of *Vejdeland*, discussed in the previous chapter, before the European Court of Human Rights). In its amicus curiae, it held that '[s]exual orientation should be treated in the same way as categories such as race, ethnicity and religion which are commonly covered by hate-speech and hate-crime laws, because sexual orientation is a characteristic that is fundamental to a person's sense of self. It is, moreover, used as a marker of group identity'.[54]

Such a principled argument (other groups are deserving protection) in the literature is complemented by a more empirical one (incitement is ongoing and should be combatted). Additional grounds than the ones currently enshrined in positive international and domestic law, this argument goes, should be considered in the event of documented acts of hateful incitement on the ground concerned. Empiricism, then, is also the yardstick to consider the multiplication of potential protective grounds here. Alexander Brown extensively considered this 'who question' and posits in this regard:

> If one ostensible goal of incitement to hatred laws is to deter words or behaviour that amount to stirring up hatred, then a basic practical requirement of any extension of such law to cover more groups must be that members of these other groups are in fact (or are likely to be) the object of words or behaviour that stirs up hatred against them. It will not suffice merely to point to the existence of at least some instances of hate speech against members of these groups; this is because not all hate speech is incitement to hatred. Thus, if one is very specifically arguing for an extension of incitement to hatred laws to cover sexual orientation, for example, it is not enough to show that instances of homophobic hate speech can be found in the media and other areas of public life ... Instead, it would be necessary to show that actual instances of the various forms of hate speech that currently surround sexual orientation, disability, body weight and age have in fact reached the level of, or qualify as, stirring up hatred on a par with other forms of stirring up hatred that are already criminalised.[55]

---

54 *Vejdeland and others* v. *Sweden*, para. 45.

55 Alexander Brown, 'The "Who?" Question in the Hate Speech Debate: Part 1: Consistency, Practical, and Formal Approaches', 29:2 *Canadian Journal of Law & Jurisprudence* (2016), pp. 275–320, at pp. 293–294 (footnotes omitted). In the second instalment, he (among other things) dispels many of the existing political or doctrinal principled arguments against extending incitement offences at least to the grounds of sexual orientation, gender identity and disability: Alexander Brown, 'The "Who?" Question in the Hate Speech

To name but one concrete example, the *travaux préparatoires* of the Swedish incitement law (which was at the heart of the *Vejdeland* case), mobilize the empirical dimension:

> [H]omosexuals constitute an exposed group which is often subjected to criminal acts because of their sexual orientation, and national socialist and other racist groups agitate against homosexuals and homosexuality as part of their propaganda. The preparatory work also stated that there were good reasons to assume that the homophobic attitude that had caused certain offenders to attack individuals on account of their sexual orientation derived from the hate, threat and inflammatory propaganda against homosexuals as a group that was spread by the majority of Nazi and other right-wing extremist groups in the country.[56]

Thus the question is whether a dynamic treaty interpretation, taking account of contemporary challenges faced by the Covenant and the rights contained therein, would warrant an inclusive reading of Article 20(2), thus including incitement on grounds of sexual orientation and gender identity, sex, disability, among other hitherto non-recognized other grounds. In respect of gender identity in particular, while it is logical to some extent – as these interventions are triggered by instances revolving around virulent anti-gay sentiments – that the just cited considerations zoom in on 'homosexuals', or more comprehensively on 'sexual orientation', the fact remains that precisely the same holds true for gender identity. Transphobic speech, as well as other forms of hateful incitement targeting gender identities, poses the same questions of human rights protection as does homophobic speech.

Applying the 'living instrument doctrine' to the Covenant, ARTICLE 19 (NGO) has proposed a more comprehensive and inclusive upgrade.[57] Specifically, this

---

Debate: Part 2: Functional and Democratic Approaches', 30:1 *Canadian Journal of Law & Jurisprudence* (2017), pp. 23–55.

56 *Vejdeland and others* v. *Sweden*, para. 19. Dutch travaux pertaining to a relevant pending Bill also extensively engage with the empirical (including societal) dimension to this debate: *Memorie van Toelichting: Wijziging van de Algemene wet gelijke behandeling en het Wetboek van Strafrecht in verband met de vervanging van de term «hetero- of homoseksuele gerichtheid» door «seksuele gerichtheid» en toevoeging aan het Wetboek van Strafrecht van de discriminatiegronden genderidentiteit, genderexpressie en geslachtskenmerken* (draft memorandum, 2020).

57 ARTICLE 19, *Responding to Hate Speech against LGBTI People: Policy Brief* (2013). See also ARTICLE 19, *Prohibiting Incitement to Discrimination, Hostility or Violence: Policy Brief* (2012), pp. 20–22.

NGO advocates for a 'coherent legal framework for prohibiting the advocacy of hatred against LGBTI people that constitutes incitement to discrimination, hostility, or violence that meets international standards in this area'.[58] It comes to the conclusion that Article 20(1) ICCPR must be understood to include the prohibited incitement grounds of sexual orientation and gender identity, reasoning that

> This interpretation would comply with the evolution of developments in human rights protections since the adoption of the ICCPR in 1977. ARTICLE 19 has also pointed out that the ICCPR was adopted before equality movements around the world made significant progress in promoting and securing human rights for all. However, it has since come to be interpreted and understood as supporting the principle of equality on a larger scale, applying to other grounds not expressly included in the treaty text, including sexual orientation and gender identity. It would also be in line with the object and purpose of international human rights law that must be interpreted "in the light of present-day conditions".[59]

This suggestion is certainly not outlandish, seeing as the UN Human Rights Committee has in the past engaged theories of dynamic / evolutionary treaty interpretation and has especially repeatedly deployed the 'living instrument' doctrine (which originates within the European Court of Human Rights). Indeed, the Committee has explicated that the 'Covenant should be interpreted as a living instrument and the rights protected under it should be applied in context and in the light of present-day conditions'.[60]

4 Comparative Law

Furthermore, state practice in parts of the world – and presumably *opinio juris*, the second requirement of customary international law – is rapidly shifting on the present point. While this practice is rapidly becoming 'extensive' it is, admittedly, hardly 'virtually uniform';[61] at least not when one considers this

58 *Ibid.*, p. 21.

59 *Ibid.*, p. 25.

60 E.g. Human Rights Committee, *Roger Judge v. Canada*, Communication No.829/1998, U.N. Doc. CCPR/C/78/D/829/1998, Views of 5 August 2002, para. 10(3).

61 Required (among other criteria) for a practice to be recognized as customary international law. International Court of Justice, *North Sea Continental Shelf*, I.C.J. Reports 1969, para. 74.

novel practice from a global perspective. There are still numerous states that have not upgraded incitement laws so as to include protection vis-à-vis the grounds of sexual orientation and gender identity. In fact, there are still many states without any relevant anti-incitement laws; some of these are opposed to incitement laws per se and allow, as a matter of constitutional principle, for higher degrees of freedom of expression.[62] Not to even mention, of course, the many dozens of countries that prohibit same-sex relationships and actively prosecute or allow persecution of persons on grounds of their sexual orientation or gender identity; needless to say, oppressive non-pluralist countries have no interest in calibrating free religious speech and equal dignity rights since they do not believe in equal dignity in the first place.

That all said, an increasing number of State parties go expressly beyond the three ICCPR-mandated prohibited grounds, but one has to take a non-global view to appreciate any comparative legal trends here. Applying a different prism, it can be concluded that strikingly uniform *regional custom* is rapidly emerging within what is called the 'WEOG' region of the United Nations (Western European and Others Group), with some additional yet more modest traces of this trend branching out into South America and elsewhere. In what follows next, a comparative law overview is presented.

At the outset of this comparative analysis section, and as further elaborated in the next chapter, it should be indicated that the scope of these forms of additional protection against incitement vary widely. More specifically, it should be noted immediately too that whereas protection against incitement on grounds of sexual orientation is making particular headway, similar societal and legal traction regarding transphobic speech and other forms of hateful incitement based on gender identity cannot be established, causing protection based on gender identity to lag behind in many countries.

Starting with a number of European examples, the Criminal Code of Denmark includes 'sexual inclination' amongst the prohibited incitement grounds.[63] French criminal law has mainstreamed 'sexual orientation', similarly, at relevant places, including throughout the criminal code chapter

---

62 See also the reservations entered by a number of states to Article 20 ICCPR. Seven states – Australia, Belgium, Luxembourg, Malta, New Zealand, United Kingdom and the United States – have deposited reservations or interpretative declarations affecting the applicability of Article 20(2) ICCPR. As the below comparative law overview indicates, some of these states have enacted incitement legislation (as the municipal level) in the face of these reservations.

63 Article 266B of the Criminal Code of Denmark; this ground was inserted as per Act No. 357 of 3 June 1987.

on 'Offences against the Physical or Psychological Integrity of the Person'.[64] Likewise, through relevant amendments,[65] in England and Wales stirring up 'hatred on the grounds of sexual orientation' is prohibited. 'Hatred', within the meaning of Irish legislation, is inclusively defined and 'means hatred against a group of persons in the State or elsewhere on account of their race, colour, nationality, religion, ethnic or national origins, membership of the travelling community or *sexual orientation*'.[66] In addition to such grounds as race or religion, the Dutch Criminal Code penalizes '[a]ny person who publicly, either verbally or in writing or through images, incites hatred of or discrimination against persons or violence against their person or property because of their ... hetero- or homosexual orientation'.[67] The *Verhetzung* (incitement) clause, to draw on another example, of the Austrian Criminal Code includes the ground of '*sexuellen Ausrichtung*'.[68] Many other European countries, including the bulk of the Western European states of WEOG, have similarly expanded in recent years their incitement or hate speech legislation so as to include (typically among other prohibited grounds) hateful incitement or hate speech against persons based on their sexual orientation.[69]

---

64 Criminal Code of France, Article 222 *et seq.*; see also Article 225 *et seq.* on punishable discrimination ('sexual morals or orientation'). Prohibited grounds inserted pursuant Law No. 2001-1066.

65 Criminal Justice and Immigration Act 2008, Section 74, which updated and expanded Part 3A of the Public Order Act 1986.

66 Prohibition of Incitement to Hatred Act [Ireland] (1989), Section 1(1) (emphasis added).

67 Criminal Code of The Netherlands, Article 137d. See also Article 137c for a separate lower-threshold insult prohibition.

68 Criminal Code of Austria, Section 283(1).

69 *E.g.* Article 233A of the General Penal Code of Iceland ('sexual inclination' inserted as per Act 135/1996); Law of 30 July 1981 on the punishment of certain acts inspired by racism or xenophobia [of Belgium], as amended pursuant Law of 10 May 2007 concerning marital status, sexual orientation, family background, financial and status (also amending the Criminal Code of Belgium in this regard); Criminal Code of Lithuania, Article 170 ('sexual orientation'); Section 16 of the Monaco Freedom of Public Expression Act No. 1.299 of 15 July 2005 ('actual or supposed sexual orientation'); Criminal Code of Norway, Article 185 ('homosexual orientation'); Article 19 of Law No. 48 [Romania] of 16 January 2002 approving Government Ordinance No. 137/2000 regarding the Prevention and Punishment of Every Form of Discrimination ('sex or sexual orientation'); Criminal Code of Slovenia, Article 297 ('sexual orientation'); see also Article 8(1) of the [Slovenian] Mass Media Act of 26 May 2001 ('sexual ... hatred'); Criminal Code of Spain, Article 510 ('gender, sexual preference'); Prevention against Discrimination Act [Bulgaria], Articles 4 and 5 ('sexual orientation'); it may be observed that Bulgaria's Criminal Code, however; omits sexual orientation from the scope of its incitement provisions (Articles 162–166); Criminal Code of Estonia, Article 151 ('sexual orientation'); Criminal Code of Finland, Section 10 of Chapter 11 ('sexual orientation' inserted into the 'Ethnic Agitation' clause as

In Australia (one of the 'Others' in the WEOG euphemism), we have to look at the state[70] level to discern incitement laws and some of these, quite similar to the cited European examples, are inclusive in terms of prohibited grounds inasmuch as these laws at least criminalize homophobic hate speech. Accordingly, in New South Wales 'homosexual vilification' is unlawful. To be precise, it is a criminal offence 'for a person, by a public act, to incite hatred towards, serious contempt for, or severe ridicule of, a person or group of persons on the ground of the homosexuality of the person or members of the group'.[71] A separate clause of this Act prohibits in similar terms transgender vilification, thus rendering protection to transgender persons against instances of hateful incitement.[72] In other parts of Australia, anti-gay speech specifically is similarly banned.[73] In New Zealand, to the contrary, there appears not to be any specific anti-incitement legislation protecting LGBT people.[74] In this legal vacuum, on at least one occasion recourse was sought within censorship regulations, which have been mobilized against an imported film that portrayed homosexuals in a prejudiced fashion.[75]

Turning to yet another part of the world,[76] Canadian criminal law – Canada is a WEOG country – includes sexual orientation in the definition of 'identifiable

---

per Law 511/2011); Law No. 4285/2014 [Greece] amending Law No. 927/1979 on Combating Race Discrimination ('sexual orientation, gender identity'); Criminal Code of Hungary, Section 332(c) ('gender identity or sexual orientation'; see also Article 171 on organized incitement); Criminal Code of Luxembourg, Article 457 (on hate speech) read in conjunction with Article 454 (on discrimination, containing the ground of '*orientation sexuelle*'); Criminal Code of Malta, Article 82A ('gender, gender identity, sexual orientation'); Criminal Code of Sweden, Chapter 16, Paragraph 8 (criminalizing 'agitation against a group', which since 2003 is interpreted inclusively so as to also mean groups defined by sexual orientation).

70 For the Federal level, see Racial Discrimination Act 1975, esp. Section 18C ('Offensive behaviour because of race, colour or national or ethnic origin'). It should be reiterated that Australia has made a reservation with respect to Article 20(2) ICCPR.

71 Anti-Discrimination Act 1977 (No. 48) [New South Wales], Section 49ZT ('public act' is separately defined in Section 49ZS).

72 *Ibid.*, Section 38S.

73 *E.g.* Anti-Discrimination Act 1998 [Tasmania], Section 19; Discrimination Act 1991 [Australian Capital Territory], Article 67A (g) ('sexuality').

74 It may be reiterated that New Zealand has deposited a reservation in relation to Article 20(2) ICCPR.

75 A series of infamous cases known as the *Living Word* cases, the final instance (with a negative result for the legal parties who sought censorship) being: Court of Appeal of New Zealand, *Living Word Distributors Ltd v. Human Rights Action Group (Wellington)*, [2000] NZCA 179; [2000] 3 NZLR 570; (2000) 18 CRNZ 81; (2000) 6 HRNZ 28, Judgment of 31 August 2000.

76 It should be reiterated that the US have made a reservation with respect to Article 20 ICCPR, which prohibition does not sit well with the free speech dictates of the First

group', one of the key elements of the law's hate propaganda provision.[77] Other North American (non-WEOG) examples of inclusive hate speech or hateful incitement legislation can be found in, for example, Mexico.[78]

Indicating that the present trend is not exclusive to WEOG although there the trend is arguably particularly pronounced, in South America too incitement and hate speech provisions that criminalize anti-LGBT speech can be identified. For instance, in the Uruguayan Criminal Code 'sexual orientation and gender identity' features as a prohibited incitement ground.[79] The laws of Colombia – together with Uruguay among the Latin American states with the most robust LGBT rights legislation in place – include 'sex or sexual orientation' in the list of grounds for incitement or hate speech.[80]

Occasionally, it takes judicial activism – in the face of legislative inaction – to prohibit anti-LGBT hate speech or hateful incitement.[81] For instance, the

---

Amendment to the US Constitution. For a more or less relevant case, see *Snyder v. Phelps*, 562 U.S. 443 (2011). The Court revoked earlier (tort-based) judicial findings and held that anti-gay 'picketing', at the hands of members of the Westboro Baptist Church, at (a reasonable distance from) funerals of fallen US soldiers is protected by the former's First Amendment right to freedom of expression. Cf., however, 2nd District Court of Appeal of Los Angeles, Judgment of 17 March 2010, finding in a 2–1 decision that anti-gay bullying via the internet of classmates does not in the circumstances of the case attract free speech protection (thus paving the way for a private law lawsuit against the bullies initiated by the parents of the victim).

77 Criminal Code of Canada, Articles 318(4) and 319. For a detailed discussion of Canadian (and other) religiously-motivated anti-LGBT hate speech cases, see Richard Moon, *Putting Faith in Hate: When Religion Is the Source or Target of Hate Speech* (Cambridge: Cambridge University Press, 2018), esp. pp. 14–16 and Ch. 5.

78 Federal Law to Prevent and Eliminate Discrimination [Mexico], Article 9(27) (on incitement to hatred) read in conjunction with Article 4 (on discriminatory acts, including the protective grounds of 'sex' and 'sexual orientation'). The law is importantly complemented by the more principled judicial approach that holds that statements that have no public value whatsoever, statements that are exclusively meant as slurs, nothing more, nothing less, are simply not covered by freedom of expression. Mexican Supreme Court, Judgment of 6 March 2013, ruling in a 3-2 decision that homophobic slurs used in publications are not covered by free speech protection.

79 Article 149 of the Criminal Code of Uruguay, inserted pursuant Law L17.677 on Incitement to Hatred, Contempt or Violence or the Commission of these Acts against Particular Individuals (*Incitación al Odio, Desprecio o Violencia o Comisión de estos Actos contra Determinadas Personas*, 2003).

80 Criminal Code of Colombia, additional grounds inserted pursuant Anti-Discrimination Law 1482/2011.

81 Some of the examples provided above may be reiterated: Mexican Supreme Court, Judgment of 6 March 2013, ruling in a 3-2 decision that homophobic slurs used in publications are not covered by free speech protection; 2nd District Court of Appeal of Los Angeles, judgment of 17 March 2010, tackling online anti-gay bullying.

Brazilian Law against Racism prohibits discriminatory acts (including speech acts) on numerous grounds, conspicuously excluding sexual orientation and gender identity.[82] Attempts to upgrade the law with a view towards including the crimes of homophobic and transphobic speech thus far have all stranded in the country's Senate. In 2019,[83] by majority decision, the Supreme Court of Brazil ruled that the exclusion of LGBT protection from the nation's anti-discrimination law was unconstitutional, thus paving the way for a legislative upgrade.

In some countries, whether in addition or instead of generic criminal law provisions on the subject, it is through media legislation that anti-LGBT hatred is combatted.[84] This typically also includes provisions urging the media not to broadcast any messages that could stereotype LGBT people or otherwise contain prejudicial views.

5 Inclusive Incitement Prohibitions: The Emerging International Practice of Mainstreaming LGBT Protection

Now, let us consider the above domestic norms and scopes of incitement prohibitions in the light of international incitement prohibitions. To what extent are these comprehensive anti-incitement laws, including prohibited grounds beyond the ICCPR-mandated grounds of 'national, racial or religious hatred', permitted or authorized by international law?

The findings in this regard of the monitoring body that oversees compliance with the ICCPR, the UN Human Rights Committee, on this very issue are naturally very significant. In that regard it should first be observed that the Human Rights Committee missed out on an excellent opportunity to definitively and generally settle this score when it adopted General Comment No. 34,[85]

82 *Lei do Crime Racial*, Law No. 7.716/1989.

83 Judgment of the Supreme Court of Brazil of 13 June 2019. The judgment followed several other judicial decisions, commencing with a February 2019 Supremo Tribunal Federal decision addressing homophobia in Brazil and including also a May 2019 judgment on the same.

84 E.g. [Slovenian] Mass Media Act of 26 May 2001, esp. Article 8(1); Television Law [Portugal], Law No. 27/2077 as amended by Law No. 2011 (including a prohibition of incitement based on sexual orientation); Law No. 6112 on the Establishment of Radio and Television Enterprises and Their Media Services [Turkey], Article 8(s), prohibiting media programmes promoting gender inequality specifically (not, however, discriminatory messages vis-à-vis LGBT people).

85 Human Rights Committee, Human Rights Committee, *General Comment 34: Article 19: Freedoms of Opinion and Expression*, CCPR/C/GC/34 (2011).

replacing the older General Comment on freedom of expression.[86] It chose not comment on the exhaustiveness of the prohibited grounds contained in Article 20(2).

The Human Rights Committee has, however, repeatedly jumped at the opportunity to comment on the quality and scope of incitement laws in the context of the state reporting procedure. In that regard, it should first of all be noted that the Committee has never reproached any country over adding additional prohibited incitement grounds of the type presented in the above overview. Moreover, the Committee has, quite the contrary, repeatedly urged states that thus far have failed to extend adequate protection to LGBT people to adopt precisely such domestic legal upgrades. For example, with respect to Jamaica the Committee expressed concern at 'reports of virulent lyrics by musicians and entertainers that incite violence against homosexuals'.[87] Jamaica was hence urged to 'bring its legislation into line with the Covenant and put an end to prejudices and the social stigmatization of homosexuality. In this regard, the State party should send a clear message that it does not tolerate any form of harassment, discrimination or violence against persons for their sexual orientation, and should ensure that individuals, who incite violence against homosexuals, are investigated, prosecuted and properly sanctioned'.[88] In this particular example, it is clear that the underlying issue is homophobic hateful incitement and the recommended solution as part of the state reporting procedure is similarly restricted: step up the fight against that particular type of extreme speech, at the minimum by having designated standards in place which can be used for a criminal law response to incitement of violence against homosexuals.

By the same logic, comprehensive standards inclusively combating hateful incitement on grounds of sexual orientation and gender identity have been recommended in instances where homophobic and transphobic and other hateful speech targeting sexual orientations and gender identities have been established to be the underlying issue. For example, in the Committee's Concluding Observations regarding Poland's performance under the ICCPR the Committee noted 'with concern a significant rise in manifestations of hate speech and intolerance directed at lesbian, gay, bisexual and transgender people' and subsequently expressed that in that light it 'regrets the absence of the provision in the Penal Code of hate speech and hate crimes based on sexual orientation

86 Human Rights Committee, *General Comment 10: Article 19*, HRI/GEN/1/Rev.6 at 132 (1983).

87 Human Rights Committee, *Concluding observations of the Human Rights Committee [Jamaica]*, CCPR/C/JAM/CO/3 (2011), para. 8.

88 *Ibid.*

or gender identity as punishable offences'.[89] Specifically, the Committee recommended Poland to 'amend the Penal Code to define hate speech and hate crimes based on sexual orientation or gender identity among the categories of punishable offences'.[90] Similar recommendations, either specifically addressing anti-gay hateful incitement or addressing both hateful incitement based on sexual orientation and also based on gender identities, have been made with respect to, among other states, Malawi[91] and Ukraine.[92]

Interestingly, also other monitoring bodies, despite the fact that the relevant treaties do not contain incitement prohibitions per se, let alone hateful incitement clauses containing sexual orientation and gender identity among the prohibited grounds, have expressed concern over states not sufficiently combatting anti-LGBT incitement. For example, the Committee on the Rights of the Child did so vis-à-vis Slovakia and Switzerland.[93] The Committee against Torture has explicitly recommended State parties to incorporate into their Criminal Codes 'an offence to punish hate crimes as acts of intolerance and

89 Human Rights Committee, *Concluding observations of the Human Rights Committee [Poland]*, CCPR/C/POL/CO/6 (2010), para. 8. Somewhat confusingly, the Committee tends to use the colloquial 'hate speech' in its concluding observations on state reports. The headings and context of the relevant excepts, however, make it clear that the reflections pertain to the incitement clause of Article 20(2) of the ICCPR; hence, the Committee is certainly not recommending low-threshold hate speech offences. The Committee uses incitement terminology more consistently in its case law ('Views').

90 *Ibid.*, also recommending such positive measures as 'intensify[ing] awarenessraising activities aimed at the police force and wider public'.

91 Human Rights Committee, *Concluding observations of the Human Rights Committee [Malawi]*, CCPR/C/MWI/CO/1 (2011), para. 7: 'The Committee is concerned about ... allegations regarding reported cases of violence and discrimination against people engaging in same-sex relationships in the State party, as well as allegations of incitement to violence against them by some public officials and authorities ... The State party should ... ensure that public officials and public authorities refrain from using language that may encourage hatred and violence against them'.

92 Human Rights Committee, *Concluding observations on the seventh periodic report of Ukraine*, CCPR/C/UKR/CO/7 (2013), para. 10: 'The Committee is concerned at reports of discrimination, hate speech and acts of violence directed at lesbian, gay, bisexual and transgender (LGBT) persons and violation of their rights to freedom of expression and assembly ... The State party should therefore state clearly and officially that it does not tolerate any form of social stigmatization of homosexuality, bisexuality or transsexuality, or hate speech, discrimination or violence against persons because of their sexual orientation or gender identity'.

93 Committee on the Rights of the Child, *Concluding observations on the combined third to fifth periodic reports of Slovakia*, CRC/C/SVK/CO/3-5 (2016), para. 15(d); *Concluding observations on the combined second to fourth periodic reports of Switzerland*, CRC/C/CHE/CO/2-4 (2015), paras. 24-25.

incitation to hatred and violence based on sexual orientation' (e.g. vis-à-vis Moldova; with comparable recommendations made to Mongolia, Norway, and Poland),[94] conspicuously omitting, though, an equivalent recommendation regarding hatred and violence based on gender identity. Occasionally yet significantly, public officials and/or states are directly reproached by UN monitoring bodies over state-instigated or otherwise official incitement of violence or discrimination against LGBT people (e.g. Holy See and Russia).[95]

Also the Universal Periodic Review mechanism, the UN human rights peer-review procedure within the Human Rights Council, has yielded conclusions to the same effect, concretely implying that states have been urging other states to upgrade their legislation with a view towards rendering explicit protection against hateful incitement on the grounds of sexual orientation and/or gender identity. In that context, France has for instance advised Cyprus to '[p]rohibit all discriminatory practices and criminalize defamation, slander and incitement to discrimination, hostility or violence, whether they are public or not, towards a person or a group of persons because of their sexual orientation'.[96] While Spain, taking a more inclusive view toward the necessary protective grounds in the battle against hateful incitement, has urged Austria to '[i]nclude a sexual orientation and gender identity perspective with regard to measures against incitement to hatred'.[97]

Further support by international human rights bodies for inclusive incitement legislation, thus upgrading the historically limited formulations of such international anti-incitement provisions as Article 20(2) ICCPR or Article

94 *E.g.* Committee against Torture, *Concluding observations of the Committee against Torture [Moldova]*, CAT/C/MDA/CO/2 (2009), para. 27. See also *Conclusions and recommendations of the Committee against Torture [Mongolia]*, CAT/C/MNG/CO/1 (2010), para. 25; *Concluding observations on the combined sixth and seventh periodic reports of Norway, adopted by the Committee at its forty-ninth session [Norway]*, CAT/C/NOR/CO/6-7 (2012), para. 21; *Conclusions and recommendations of the Committee against Torture [Poland]*, CAT/C/POL/CO/4 (2007), para. 20.

95 Committee on the Rights of the Child, *Concluding observations on the second periodic report of the Holy See*, CRC/C/VAT/CO/2 (2014), para. 25: 'the Committee is concerned about past statements and declarations made by the Holy See on homosexuality, which contribute to the social stigmatization of and violence against lesbian, gay, bisexual, and transgender adolescents and children raised by same sex couples'. See also para. 26 (ibid.) for the Committee's recommendations in this regard. Human Rights Committee, *Concluding observations of the Human Rights Committee [Russia]*, CCPR/C/RUS/CO/6 (2009), para. 27.

96 Human Rights Council, *Report of the Working Group on the Universal Periodic Review: Cyprus*, A/HRC/13/7 (2010), para. 27.

97 Human Rights Council, *Report of the Working Group on the Universal Periodic Review: Austria*, A/HRC/17/8 (2011), para. 93.32.

4 ICERD, may be charted. Notably, the United Nations High Commissioner for Human Rights has emphasized the 'obligation', which flows from the UN mechanisms, to take 'legislative and other measures to prohibit, investigate and prosecute all acts of targeted, hate-motivated violence and incitement to violence directed at LGBT and intersex persons, and to provide remedy to victims and protection against reprisals'.[98] Expressing concern at 'inflammatory rhetoric' used in such states as Belarus, Gambia and Honduras, the High Commissioner has found that '[s]uch language is used by some political and community leaders to promote negative stereotypes, stir up prejudice and harass particular individuals, especially during electoral periods'.[99] In its report, these findings cumulate in the recommendation that states address violence by '[p]rohibiting incitement of hatred and violence on the grounds of sexual orientation and gender identity, and holding to account those responsible for related hate speech'.[100]

In addition to the treaty-based monitoring bodies and the charter-based and other political UN bodies and offices mentioned so far, a host of additional international and regional instruments as well as recommendations or other workings by international bodies, governmental and non-governmental, can be cited for additional support to inclusive readings of international incitement prohibitions, thus rendering protection to the grounds of sexual orientation and – less frequently, the caveat must be repeated – gender identity. In what remains of the chapter, a few final examples will be highlighted.

Similar to some domestic laws in this area, in specific relation to the media some instruments promote speech prohibitions of a somewhat lower threshold than do proper incitement bans. Specifically, the mass and or commercial (audio-visual) media are pursuant to such instruments forbidden from broadcasting messages that discriminate against or stereotype sexual orientations or gender identities. For instance, the EU Audiovisual Media Services Directive provide that commercial communications shall not 'include or promote any discrimination based on sex … or sexual orientation'.[101] Other international

98 United Nations High Commissioner for Human Rights, *Discrimination and violence against individuals based on their sexual orientation and gender identity*, A/HRC/29/23 (2015), para. 11. See also the earlier *Discriminatory laws and practices and acts of violence against individuals based on their sexual orientation and gender identity: Report of the United Nations High Commissioner for Human Rights*, A/HRC/19/41 (2011).

99 *Ibid.* (2015), para. 33.

100 *Ibid.*, para 78(d).

101 EU Audiovisual Media Services Directive, Article 9(1)(c)(ii).

benchmarks have made sure to include gender identity among the protective grounds in this regard.[102]

The UN Special Rapporteur on the promotion and protection of the right to freedom of opinion and expression has noted that the fight against discrimination of persons based on their sexual orientation or gender identity must go hand in hand with tackling incitement to hatred based on those same grounds.[103] More specifically, this Rapporteur has expressed support for legal initiatives that step up the fight against (inciting) homophobic, transphobic and misogynistic messages.[104]

Civil society, too, has expressed ample support for inclusively interpreting existing incitement prohibitions. Examples already referred to include the *amicus* interventions by Interrights and free speech NGO ARTICLE 19 in relevant (European) cases on homophobic hate speech. Other non-governmental momentum certainly came in the form of the 2006 *Yogyakarta Principles*,[105] a set of principles on the application of international human rights law in relation to sexual orientation and gender identity drafted and adopted by international human rights experts, which interestingly mainstreams anti-incitement efforts with the *right to security of the person*. That is, while the Principles' freedom of expression clause only very generally stipulates that 'States shall ... [e]nsure that the exercise of freedom of opinion and expression does not violate the rights and freedoms of persons of diverse sexual orientations and gender identities',[106] Principle 5 on security of the person provides that states must take 'all necessary legislative measures to impose appropriate criminal penalties for violence, threats of violence, incitement to violence and related

102 The Yogyakarta Principles stipulate that the 'mass media avoid the use of stereotypes in relation to sexual orientation and gender identity' and more specifically provides that States must '[e]nsure that the outputs and the organisation of media that is State-regulated is pluralistic and non-discriminatory in respect of issues of sexual orientation and gender identity'. *Yogyakarta Principles: Principles on the application of international human rights law in relation to sexual orientation and gender identity* (2007), resp. Additional Recommendation O and Principle 19(B).

103 Special Rapporteur on the promotion and protection of the right to freedom of opinion and expression, *Promotion and protection of the right to freedom of opinion and expression*, A/67/357 (2012), para. 75, with further concern expressed at anti-LGBT incitement by politicians, the media and religious leaders at para. 27.

104 *Report of the Special Rapporteur on the promotion and protection of the right to freedom of opinion and expression, Frank La Rue [Mission to Italy]*, A/HRC/26/30/Add.3 (2014), paras. 66 and 88.

105 *Yogyakarta Principles: Principles on the application of international human rights law in relation to sexual orientation and gender identity* (2007).

106 Yogyakarta Principles, Principle 19(E).

harassment, based on the sexual orientation or gender identity of any person or group of persons, in all spheres of life, including the family'.[107]

6 Concluding Remarks

In conclusion, an increasing number of states adopt inclusive anti-incitement laws covering the grounds of sexual orientation and gender identity. Also international monitoring bodies, independent experts, intergovernmental bodies are increasingly vocal and united in favouring a reading of international anti-incitement standards that includes protection against hateful incitement on grounds of sexual orientation and gender identity. The European Court of Human Rights, but only through its very recent (2020) jurisprudence has gone furthest in this regard, by actually spelling out (vis-à-vis individual state parties) the Convention's implicit duties to protect, through criminal law, homosexuals against hateful incitement and to investigate homophobic hate speech specifically. Future cases brought to Strasbourg on transphobic and other hate speech on grounds of gender identity will reveal whether the Court is willing to identify concomitant Convention duties, protecting transgenders, intersex persons, and others. This certainly cannot be ruled out: The current omission has to do with the ad hoc and reactive nature of the European Court's findings in the present regard. While it is the Strasbourg Court that sets the tone here, in the absence of designated Convention standards on extreme speech, the Court is in so doing dependent on the cases being brought before it. Seeing the Court's steadfast approach in the homophobic hate speech case of *Beizaras and Levickas v. Lithuania*, the first landmark transphobic hate speech decision to be handed down by the Court may be a matter of time.

UN treaty monitoring bodies' Concluding Observations are also increasingly outspoken on the subject and suggest that international human rights law must be interpreted as rendering protection to LGBT people against hateful incitement. With respect to the ICCPR specifically, it is certainly tempting to argue that inclusive incitement legislation flows compulsorily from the Covenant. The Human Rights Committee, however, hitherto comes to this conclusion in an ad hoc fashion. That is, wherever the absence of protection for LGBT people from acts of hateful incitement is glaring in concrete instances the Committee mobilizes the Covenant to remedy this. It has not yet, for example as per a General Comment, made a general instruction to State parties to the ICCPR

107 Yogyakarta Principles, Principle 5.

to adopt and implement the desired upgrade. The Human Rights Committee's position is far from insignificant, though. In the face of the domestically-instigated development whereby states have, in tandem with advancing societal emancipation in these parts of the world, boldly extended anti-incitement protection to LGBT people beyond the literal terms of the Covenant, the UN Human Rights Committee has not been digging in its heels. Quite the contrary, it has rather taken this development as its cue to expedite the same trend, thus actually steering on further proliferation of inclusive incitement legislation rendering protection to LGBT people.

It is fair to say that, from a global perspective, we cannot establish uniform state practice aimed at eradicating anti-LGBT incitement and hate speech, but at the regional (WEOG) level we may safely speak in terms of rapidly emerging custom to that very effect. Seeing, however, the strong interplay and dynamics between the just indicated swiftly advancing authoritative views on the part of international monitoring bodies and this emerging regional commitment to inclusive protection against hateful incitement, it may well be a matter of time before the regional nature of the said custom is all but immaterial. After all, monitoring bodies are perfectly positioned and mandated to incorporate the need to face contemporary challenges into their understanding of international human rights law provisions, and they are indeed increasingly doing just that.

That all said, it should at the same time be noted that we are dealing with shifting understandings of positive international law and especially the legislative ramifications that flow from this body of law – while this chapter has charted a certain degree of momentum in the latter regard, a more universal degree of enforcement informed by the same sense of urgency is numerous hurdles away. Indeed, countries that do not believe in eradicating discrimination against persons on grounds of sexual orientation and gender identity in the first place will not be jumping at this shift in interpretation in the area of combating incitement and hate speech.

At the very least, then, the developments charted in this chapter may function to embolden judges and human rights bodies, international and domestic, to read into anti-incitement standards and human rights obligations the protective grounds of sexual orientation and gender identity.

Nevertheless, it may well remain important for international monitoring bodies to significantly steer that process by rendering expert-based guidance, lest anti-incitement laws and policies become subject to fragmentation with differing degrees of protection as a result. The next chapter addresses lessons learnt as well as concerns caused by emerging practice in this area, zooming into legislative examples in more detail.

CHAPTER 4

The Scope of the Anti-LGBT Incitement Offence

Lessons from Comparative Law

1 Introduction

The previous chapter identified a number of state laws, arguing there is a (regional) trend to extend protection to LGBT people against hateful incitement. From the international law, authoritative benchmarks and jurisprudence review, it transpired that international law certainly permits anti-LGBT incitement prohibitions and increasingly international monitoring bodies are recommending if not strictly requiring them to be in place.

That said, international law – by way of monitoring bodies or experts – has not gone quite as far as to dictate one exact formulation of the prohibition of incitement against LGBT people. This chapter discusses concrete formulations with a view to identifying 'good practice' as well as challenges and ostensible pitfalls.

2 Inclusive Anti-Incitement Laws: Progress and Challenges

The dynamics between international and domestic law, as a result, can be appreciated as follows: one the one hand, domestic incitement standards that have already incorporated LGBT+ protection can be deemed to be standard-bearers of LGBT+ equal dignity rights. On the other hand, if such progressive development through domestic protection remains too much in the vanguard there is a risk not only of unchecked fragmentation of (domestic implementation of) international incitement standards, but also in theory of incitement standards that overstep the mark from an international human rights perspective. Think of incitement standards with too low thresholds, unduly restricting freedom of expression, including incitement standards that unduly restrict free religious speech specifically.[1]

1 The next chapter zooms in on this question of interplay between free religious speech and protection against hateful incitement.

 DOI:10.1163/9789004458864_005

Furthermore, in the absence of legal guidance by international monitoring bodies, there is a risk that incitement standards – albeit at least adopted in this area in the first place – are framed in *too limited* a fashion. Indeed, in the absence of clear guidance states could cherry-pick additional protective grounds, expressly ignoring LGBT protection. That is to say, some countries do go beyond the grounds mentioned in Article 20(2) of the ICCPR but omit the grounds that form the subject of this book. Accordingly, Turkey and Ukraine,[2] while criminalizing hateful incitement on grounds of sex, have not prohibited incitement on grounds of sexual orientation and gender identity.[3] While protection against incitement of violence or discrimination against women is to be applauded since this remedies yet another historical omission caused by Article 20(2) of the ICCPR, selectively going beyond the terms of the latter provision makes the precarious status of protective measures vis-à-vis the grounds of sexual orientation and gender identity all the more striking, if not to say conspicuous.

Another risk of fragmentation occurs *within* the protective grounds of sexual orientation and gender identity. States could decide to render protection to some aspects of equality on grounds sexual orientation and gender identity but not to other elements. An exclusive protective focus on homosexuality, for instance, may not sufficiently cover other vulnerable sexual orientations. Or, to name another example, the inclusion of transgenderism as a protective ground is an important legal extension clearly, but if legislatively literally referred to like that, it may serve in practice to exclude for example intersex people from protection against incitement.

In the present context of fragmented practise, it may be pointed out that the "T+" in LGBT+ rights protection is arguably triggering the least attention by legislators, which are often-times not even-handed enough when it comes

2 Criminal Code of Ukraine, Article 161 (list of prohibited grounds including 'sex', but omitting 'sexual orientation'). The latter law does open-endedly include the phrase 'or other characteristics', making it viable to read into the law the ground of sexual orientation as a prohibited ground. The Ukrainian judiciary, however, has not yet done so while the Ukrainian Parliament, moreover, has repeatedly declared itself against extending LGBT and gender identity protection through hate crime legislation. Criminal Code of Turkey, Article 216(2) ('public degradation' on grounds of 'gender'); see also Law No. 6112 on the Establishment of Radio and Television Enterprises and Their Media Services, Article 8(s) (prohibiting media programmes promoting gender inequality).

3 In the case of Turkey, this omission has been belied, partly, by jurisprudence of its Constitutional Court which in a case in which homosexuals were referred to as 'perverts' by a lawyer convicted the latter for hate speech. Constitutional Court of Turkey, *Sinem Hun*, Case No. 2013/5356, Judgment of 8 May 2014.

to promoting equal rights and protection on grounds of sexual orientation *and* gender identity. This general concern is very much visible when measures combating homophobic speech are compared and contrasted with measures combating transphobic speech and other hateful speech targeting gender identities. The latter measures are first of all much more scarce and even when and where in place, instances of transphobic and other hateful speech targeting gender identities are in practise very often not investigated on a par with homophobic speech, suggesting that authorities do not take the former issue seriously at all, or at least not as serious as the latter issue. Indeed, the overwhelming majority of instances that make it to court cases as discussed in the present book concern instances of homophobic hate speech and incitement.[4] This is not because transphobic speech occurs any less, but because societal acceptance is pacing behind, and also jurisprudence is pacing behind because there is no access to justice on this issue, or where there is access, investigative efforts remain faulty or half-hearted.[5]

Existing laws rendering protection to the LGBT+ community against incitement do not to use that very acronym. Existing formulations can be categorized along a spectrum of inclusiveness. Among the more inclusive anti-incitement laws in existence in the present regard are the ones of Malta (including the protective grounds of 'gender, gender identity, sexual orientation')[6] and Uruguay ('sexual orientation or gender identity').[7] The common formulation 'sexual

4 Exceptions include e.g. *R. (Miller) v. The College of Policing & The Chief Constable of Humberside*, [2020] EWHC 225 (Admin), Judgment of 14 February 2019, with respect to which it may well be argued that the transphobic nature of the impugned tweets was not sufficiently recognized and Miller's claims that he is merely 'gendercritical' or that his tweets were in service of an important public debate on the issue of sex versus gender were rather uncritically accepted. Further on this, see Chapter 5.

5 E.g. ECRI, *Compilation of ECRI Country Reports Recommendations Pertaining to LGBT Persons (Fifth Monitoring Cycle)*, underscoring deficiencies in the law enforcement department in numerous European countries on the matter of transphobic and homophobic crimes, including hate speech crimes.

6 Criminal Code of Malta, Article 82A. Malta, paradoxically, is not only a state with constitutional references to the importance of the Catholic Church and a population overwhelmingly nominally adhering to the same, it is also one of the States with an express reservation in place vis-à-vis Article 20 ICCPR, stipulating that the country 'reserves the right not to introduce any legislation for the purposes of article 20'.

7 Article 149 of the Criminal Code of Uruguay; see also e.g. the Greek Law No. 4285/2014 amending Law No. 927/1979 on Combating Race Discrimination ('sexual orientation, gender identity'); Criminal Code of Hungary, Section 332(c) ('gender identity or sexual orientation'). On the Greek Law, see Ioanna Tourkochoriti, 'The New Regulation against Hate Speech in Greece: Strength and Weaknesses', *CritCom* (20 February 2015).

orientation and sex/gender',[8] by contrast, is obviously not quite as inclusive as the versions that insist on sexual orientation and gender *identity*. Such laws, hence, are dependent upon inclusive judicial interpretation to extend protection to transgenders, intersex persons, among other gender identities.

Australia's (regional) homosexual and transgender vilification laws are quite inclusive too.[9] While protection of the ground of 'homosexuality' has been deemed, by some within the LGBT+ community, as a male-oriented and hence exclusive notion (the same goes for 'gay', which however is not typically used as a legislative notion, while it is at times as a judicial one), legally the term is typically understood to render inclusive protection to the LGB community. From the perspective of gender identity and inclusive protection against hateful incitement, an exclusive focus on transphobic speech could be problematic in practice, as it is unclear whether such a notion renders protection to non-binary gender identities not characterized by transgenderism, notably inter- and asexuality. A South African hate crime bill,[10] *Prevention and Combating of Hate Crimes and Hate Speech*, is striking for spelling out that sex includes intersex.[11] Additionally, 'gender', 'gender identity', 'sexual orientation', are all covered as protective grounds.[12]

---

8 *E.g.* Article 19 of Law No. 48 [Romania] of 16 January 2002 approving Government Ordinance No. 137/2000 Regarding the Prevention and Punishment of Every Form of Discrimination ('sex or sexual orientation'); Criminal Code of Spain, Article 510 ('gender, sexual preference'); Criminal Code of Lithuania, Article 170 ('sex, sexual orientation'); Federal Law to Prevent and Eliminate Discrimination [Mexico], Article 4 ('sex' … 'sexual orientation').

9 *E.g.* Anti-Discrimination Act 1977 (No. 48) [New South Wales], Sections 38S and 49ZT. Tasmania's comprehensive (decentral) law should also be mentioned here since it does not only mention 'sexual orientation' but makes sure to add 'the gender identity or intersex variations of sex characteristics of the person or any member of the group'. Anti-Discrimination Act 1998 [Tasmania], Section 19 (c and e). Cf. e.g. Discrimination Act 1991 [Australian Capital Territory], Article 67A (g) ('sexuality') and (d) ('intersex status').

10 Pending for years as a result of expert, media and civil society concerns over the question whether free speech might be curbed too much. E.g. Wendy Isaack, *South African Move on Hate Speech a Step Too Far* (Human Rights Watch, news article of 21 February 2017, available at <https://www.hrw.org/news/2017/02/21/south-african-move-hate-speech-step-too-far>). The Ministry of Justice issued a response to these concerns, yet the bill remains pending. Department of Justice and Constitutional Development (South Africa), *Response to the concerns raised regarding the Prevention and Combating of Hate Crimes and Hate Speech Bill* (1 November 2016).

11 Prevention and Combating of Hate Crimes and Hate Speech Bill (not entered into force yet), Article 4(1)(a)(ii)(nn).

12 *Ibid.*, at Article 4(1)(a)(hh) and (oo) respectively.

By contrast, Dutch law is – a clear example of 'dialectics of lead'[13] – striking for its restricted formulation since it merely refers to hatred based on one's 'hetero- or homosexual orientation'.[14] This formulation is obviously non-inclusive in as far as a fair number of other sexual orientations or gender identities (e.g. transgenderism, inter- or asexuality) appear not to be covered if one were to follow the strict letter of the law. It should be pointed out, though, that at the time of writing the Dutch legislator is considering changing the law and to replace 'hetero- or homosexual orientation' with 'sexual orientation' (*seksuele gerichtheid*) and to add in relevant places of Dutch equality law and Dutch criminal law the grounds of 'sex characteristics, gender identity, gender expression' (*hun geslachtskenmerken, genderidentiteit of genderexpressie*),[15] thus potentially in one fell swoop turning Dutch incitement standards from seriously lacking behind to being among the more inclusive ones in the near future. The legal memorandum pertaining to the pending amendment explains that the choice for 'sexual orientation' is informed by international developments making this the standard and most inclusive notion; while the insertion of gender identities into the law is crucial to fill a legal void and to

13 Dutch LGBT rights protection, including generic equal rights, marriage rights, eradication of work-related and other discrimination, was at some point in time pioneering. The language – a result of historical political, societal and academic debates – used in some of the relevant laws is decades' old and is, hence, currently running out of step with contemporary advances in socio-legal theory – the very reason why, see *infra* and next footnotes, the legal formulae are currently being revisited. Further on the historical rationale behind the terminology chosen, see Wibren van der Burg, *Het Democratisch Perspectief: Een Verkenning van de Normatieve Grondslagen der Democratie* (Arnhem: Gouda Quint, 1991), pp. 171–172 (see also the sources there cited).

14 Criminal Code of The Netherlands, Article 137d.

15 *Wijziging van de Algemene wet gelijke behandeling en het Wetboek van Strafrecht in verband met de vervanging van de term «hetero- of homoseksuele gerichtheid» door «seksuele gerichtheid» en toevoeging aan het Wetboek van Strafrecht van de discriminatiegronden genderidentiteit, genderexpressie en geslachtskenmerken* (2020 amendment, pending). At the time of writing, the addition is to be inserted in provision 137e (disseminating hatred) of the Criminal Code, but not into the more robust incitement provision of article 137d (incitement to hatred and discrimination). Neither the amendment nor the legal memorandum make clear why, except for one unconvincing brief mention in the latter that these grounds are currently also protected through the latter article by way of the word '*geslacht*' (sex) – a remark that appears to defeat the purpose of the whole legal upgrade. *Memorie van Toelichting: Wijziging van de Algemene wet gelijke behandeling en het Wetboek van Strafrecht in verband met de vervanging van de term «hetero- of homoseksuele gerichtheid» door «seksuele gerichtheid» en toevoeging aan het Wetboek van Strafrecht van de discriminatiegronden genderidentiteit, genderexpressie en geslachtskenmerken* (draft memorandum, 2020), para. 3.

step up protection of persons (among other things against discrimination and hatred) who fall outside the traditional binary frame of female-male sexes.[16]

In one particular respect, however, the current Dutch prohibition may be said to have been inclusive since the standard clearly works both ways, i.e. covering both anti-gay and anti-hetero speech acts. Dutch incitement and hate speech laws, on this point, are comparable to British ones, as the latter defines 'hatred on the grounds of sexual orientation' as 'hatred against a group of persons defined by reference to sexual orientation (*whether towards persons of the same sex, the opposite sex or both*)'.[17] Most incitement laws that include sexual orientation are implicitly or explicitly (especially laws discussed before on eradicating homophobic hate speech specifically)[18] akin to minority protection laws. Strictly speaking, some of those formulations imply that anti-straight incitement is legal. On the one hand, this stands to reason and can be historically explained. While the latter type of speech is a rare phenomenon, the relevant norms have emerged to tackle a real issue, namely incitement against more vulnerable groups. On the other hand, the rationale of these incitement laws is to promote equality and legal protection regardless of one's sexual orientation; hence, keeping the option of protection open vis-à-vis all potential forms of incitement is advisable. It is, after all, in the application of the standard that risk factors and vulnerability of the targeted group help pinpoint whether actual interference with free speech is merited or not (see also the next chapter for further discussion of the application of incitement provisions).

A number of prohibitions emphasize the fact that it should not matter whether the hatred is aimed at an actual or an imagined or supposed or projected type of sexual orientation.[19] This certainly stands to reason. After all, it should not matter, for the incitement to be a criminal act, that the person who is subject to hateful abuse actually belongs to the sexual orientation targeted. A species of hate crimes, hateful incitement is triggered by the hatred on the part of the hater, whether misdirected or not.

---

16 *Ibid.*

17 Public Order Act 1986, Section 29AB (S. 29AB inserted as per Criminal Justice and Immigration Act 2008 (c. 4), ss. 74, 153(7), Sch. 16 para. 4; S.I. 2010/712, art. 2(d)).

18 In addition to the Australian examples discussed before, see e.g. Criminal Code of Norway, Article 185 ('homosexual orientation').

19 E.g. Section 16 of the Monaco Freedom of Public Expression Act No. 1.299 of 15 July 2005 ('actual *or supposed* sexual orientation').

3 Concluding Remarks

While in the previous chapter it was demonstrated that advancing state practice has been a triggering factor for international monitoring bodies to start moving on the issue of anti-LGBT incitement, zooming in on relevant domestic positive law shows fairly fragmented patterns and degrees of inclusivity. The cherry-picking accusation may not always be fair, since states need to stay attuned to societal developments. The explanation for differences in recognition, hence, may have to do with the state of societal acceptance of the various protective grounds, something that may differ from country to country, or even from locality to locality. And yet, while an explanation perhaps when scrutinizing state practice, the very same issue of varying degrees of recognition also points to vulnerability, especially for widely non-protected or even non-recognized gender identities. As such, and especially taking into account questions of intersectionality,[20] that is, the fact that overlapping sexual orientation and gender identity characteristics make for extreme vulnerability, such factual non-recognition at the same time serves as a principled argument for expanding protection. In that sense, there is an important role to play for international monitoring bodies to take stock and co-steer the process of progressively developing the protective grounds.

With respect to our final motivating question of how to combat anti-LGBT incitement while at the same time promoting free religious speech discourse, it is observed that few states seek to address that delicate matter through the incitement legislation itself. In the next chapter we will see that most states with both inclusive incitement legislation and religious freedom safeguards in place leave the precise balancing task to the judiciary, not the legislator.

20 The United Nations Division for the Advancement of Women provides the following definition: 'The idea of "intersectionality" seeks to capture both the structural and dynamic consequences of the interaction between two or more forms of discrimination or systems of subordination'. DAW, *Gender and Racial Discrimination: Report of the Expert Group Meeting* (2000). See also Kimberlé Crenshaw, 'Mapping the Margins: Intersectionality, Identity Politics, and Violence against Women of Color', 46:6 *Stanford Law Review* (1991), pp. 1241–1299. For a discussion of intersectionality within hate speech discourse, see Nazila Ghanea, 'Intersectionality and the Spectrum of Racist Hate Speech: Proposals to the UN Committee on the Elimination of Racial Discrimination', 32:4 *Human Rights Quarterly* (2013), pp. 935–954.

CHAPTER 5

Combating Anti-LGBT Incitement While Promoting Religious Freedom

Balances and Threshold Questions

1 Introduction

In light of the trends described in Chapter 3 and the emerging duty to prohibit hateful incitement against LGBT people, our final and most complex question is how to square that cause – stepping up the fight against homophobia, transphobia and other phobias related to sexual orientations and gender identities – with the duty to protect freedom of expression generally and free religious speech discourse specifically. Implicit in that question is of course the controversial issue as to whether – under what circumstances and to what extent – religious freedom should be regarded a legal defence against incitement and hate speech charges.

Little international guidance exists on this delicate matter. Legal standards, general comments or other benchmarks, and relevant jurisprudence are scant and do not engage the above questions directly or extensively. International law contains freedom of expression and freedom of religion standards and international law contains anti-incitement standards that, we saw in Chapter 3, are increasingly geared towards protecting the LGBT+ community. International law does not indicate in minute detail how to resolve potential tensions between the various formidable stakes.

That is not to say that international law is completely silent. From the above chapters, especially Chapter 3, we do know that with respect to the issue of conflicting rights resulting from extreme speech international human rights law has left a significant and unique mark. This is one of the few conflicting rights scenarios international human rights law has sought to settle in an a priori fashion: through prohibiting the most extreme type of extreme speech, namely hateful incitement to discrimination or violence. Yet, the generic statement made by Article 20(2) of the ICCPR – any advocacy of hatred that constitutes incitement to discrimination, hostility or violence shall be prohibited by law – and related international human rights provisions do not provide a wholesale answer to the questions raised about conflicting rights for a number of reasons.

 | DOI:10.1163/9789004458864_006

International anti-incitement norms (enshrined in ICERD and ICCPR) oblige state parties to have incitement prohibitions in place; however, as far as their application is concerned, any actually imposed restrictions (verdicts, sanctions, penalties, fines, prison sentences, dismissals or other repercussions in the non-criminal sphere) must comply with the rules of necessity and proportionality generally applicable to limitation of free speech.[1] Furthermore, we know from international human rights law that *criminal law sanctions* particularly must be deployed as a last resort.[2]

What makes the legal framework particularly complicated is the absence of black-and-white or zero-sum rules. Again, even if a speech act amounts to incitement, not in all instances the same kind of penalty is permitted, given the necessity principle. And if a speech act does not amount to incitement within the meaning of international incitement prohibitions, some monitoring bodies may still permit restrictions under circumstances in the light of the regular limitations enshrined within freedom of expression standards. Naturally, there is a wide category of speech that falls short of incitement but that does risk affecting the freedoms or reputation of LGBT people. Indeed, monitoring bodies like the European Court of Human Rights and ECRI have permitted interferences with freedom of speech in cases that do not revolve around incitement. Consequently, according to those readings of international human rights law, there may be speech acts that fall short of the incitement threshold and hence states are not *obliged* to combat such speech through anti-incitement standards, but at the same time states may under circumstances be *permitted* to limit those same speech acts under the regular limitation clauses pertaining to freedom of expression, always subject of course to the same necessity principle. The conclusion that a speech act does not qualify as hateful incitement does not suffice, especially the European Court of Human Rights has implied time and again in its case-law sanctioning rather low-threshold interferences

1 Human Rights Committee, *General Comment No. 34: Article 19: Freedoms of Opinion and Expression*, CCPR/C/GC/34 (2011), paras. 50-52.

2 E.g. European Court of Human Rights, *Beizaras and Levickas v. Lithuania*, Application No. 41288/15, Judgment of 14 January 2020, para. 111; *Rabat Plan of Action on the prohibition of advocacy of national, racial or religious hatred that constitutes incitement to discrimination, hostility or violence*, Conclusions and recommendations emanating from the four regional expert workshops organised by OHCHR in 2011, adopted by experts in Rabat, Morocco on 5 October 2012, para. 34 (endorsed by the UN OHCHR, *Report of the United Nations High Commissioner for Human Rights on the expert workshops on the prohibition of incitement to national, racial or religious hatred* (A/HRC/22/17/Add.4, 2013)).

('defamation', 'insult', and so on) with free speech,[3] to render the speech act 'protected speech' status.

Be that as it may, with respect to the issue of incitement – and that is what makes this phenomenon unique under international human rights law – we know that the response (eradication by way of prevention and through mandated responses including penalties) thereto is not merely a permitted one, but a compulsory one. The language of the international human rights conventions was at least always clear on that score, presently the jurisprudence of the European Court of Human Rights is bringing the Convention in line with that UN approach to dealing with the most extreme type of speech (as narrated in chapter 3).

For the time being, existing international and especially state practise on eradicating anti-LGBT hateful incitement remains very much preoccupied with the treatment of extreme speech in court, with 'extreme speech on trial' if you will, and the reactive and very much binary legal question whether we are dealing with protected speech or prohibited speech that may result in criminal penalties. Admittedly, this is not surprising in the light of the fact that legal doctrine is presently in the very process of coming to terms with this category of speech; indeed, as narrated in this book, up until recently it was not clear whether anti-LGBT hatred fell into the category of prohibited type of incitement in the first place. Initial brushstrokes in this area, hence, are predictably fairly rough and rigid. The jurisprudential conclusions render certain extreme speech acts as protected, while others are deemed criminally liable. The judgments at hand, typically, do not indicate what else a state could or should have done in the face of virulent hate speech or incitement, including intolerant speech acts that fall short of the applicable criminal thresholds. Yet, it is important not to lose sight of the fact that the toolkit for dealing with extreme speech is more comprehensive than criminal law-based approaches per se. Think especially of preventative ('positive') measures in the area of education, sensitization, and awareness-raising (see Chapter 6).

For our present discussion, this means that finding issue with a concrete judgment by which someone was convicted of extreme speech does not suggest

3 The Strasbourg Court's sanctioning of overly low-threshold restrictions has been criticized, including by the present author. E.g. Jeroen Temperman, 'Blasphemy and the European Court of Human Rights: A Small Step Forward, A Giant Leap Back', in Philip Czech, Lisa Heschl, Karin Lukas, Manfred Nowak and Gerd Oberleitner (eds.), *European Yearbook on Human Rights* (Cambridge: Intersentia, 2019), pp. 221–236; and Jeroen Temperman, 'Blasphemy, Defamation of Religions & Human Rights Law', 26(4) *Netherlands Quarterly of Human Rights* (2008), pp. 517–545.

that the state should have done nothing in the face of intolerant acts at stake. Such criticism is limited to the particular use of the criminal law avenue in the case at hand, while the state's wider extreme speech policy may be subject to separate praise of criticism. Reversely, the conclusion that a court applies a robust incitement test – whatever the precise judicial outcome – does not inform us as to the soundness of the respective country's overall policies concerning intolerant speech, speech targeting reputations and speech affecting the equal dignity rights of persons and groups.

2 Against Sweeping Scripture Defences

With respect to the specific issue of religiously-motivated hatred some, albeit little, guidance can be distilled from the international plane. Religious freedom, the lesson appears to be, is not quite accepted as an absolute trump to charges of hateful incitement. In the case of *Ross* concerning a dismissed anti-Semitic school teacher, the applicant claimed that his statements merely represented 'conflicts between Judaism and Christianity' and that he had made them in 'defence of the Christian religion'.[4] Canada's response was that Ross had merely 'cloaked his views under the guise of the Christian faith'.[5] The Human Rights Committee does not get to the bottom of Ross's exact religious views, but by considering that the facts of the case showed that 'Jewish communities' right to be protected from religious hatred'[6] was at stake and that the restrictions imposed on Ross's freedom of (religious) speech were prescribed by law,[7] legitimate ('[s]uch restrictions also derive support from the principles reflected in article 20(2) of the Covenant'), and necessary 'to protect the right or reputations of persons of the Jewish faith',[8] it is clear that applicable freedom of religious speech in the circumstances of this case did in any event not trump the protection Canada needed to render to Jews to be protected against hatred. Accordingly, freedom of religious speech is a factor to reckon with but it does not, when invoked, automatically immunize a person from interferences with one's free speech.

4 Human Rights Committee, *Malcolm Ross v. Canada*, Communication No. 736/1997, CCPR/C/70/D/736/1997 (2000), Views of 18 October 2000, at para. 2.1; see also paras. 4.2, 5.2, 5.4 and 7.3.
5 *Ibid.*, at para. 6.5; see also para. 6.4.
6 *Ibid.*, at para. 11.5.
7 *Ibid.*, at para. 11.5.
8 *Ibid.*, at para. 11.6.

It is against the background of this (scant) international guidance that in the present section a case will be made against overly rigid a priori and in abstracto balances, whether legislative or judicial, between the relevant rights of religious speech freedom and equal dignity rights and in favour of case-by-case and above all context-dependent judicial calibration of these potentially conflicting rights. Let us first consider a number of alternative approaches, which in lieu of more detailed guidance at the international plane are derived again from state practice.

Interestingly, some domestic anti-incitement laws make sure to provide religious freedom defences more or less explicitly. For example, the Criminal Code of Canada stipulates that '[n]o person shall be convicted of [the offence of wilful promotion of hatred] ... if, in good faith, the person expressed or attempted to establish by an argument an opinion on a religious subject or an opinion based on a belief in a religious text'.[9] Australian legislation at the state level of New South Wales provides that while homosexual and transgender vilification are generally unlawful, this shall not be the case for 'a public act, done reasonably and in good faith, for academic, artistic, *religious instruction*, scientific or research purposes or for other purposes in the public interest, including discussion or debate about and expositions of any act or matter'.[10] While the formulations of these legal caveats differ somewhat in terms of nature and scope and hence *impact* on the present debate, one common denominator appears to be the principle of good faith. This is not unimportant, as it indicates that, yes, a religious freedom defence is explicitly foreseen, but the invocation thereof must be bona fide. Hence, the caveat within the caveat makes the defence a non-absolute or contingent one. Abuse of the religious context of the speech act in the shape of religious discourse not abiding by the good faith principle, presumably including unequivocal calls for hatred, are not necessarily shielded.

Where this has not been expressly foreseen by the legislator, the judiciary may in actual practice carve out a religious freedom defence in a jurisprudential fashion. Notable examples include (*mutatis mutandis*) the Dutch *el-Moumni* case and the Swedish *Åke Green* case.

Imam el-Moumni[11] was indicted for publicly insulting homosexuals and for inciting hatred, discrimination or violence against them on grounds of their sexual orientation.[12] While the second count could not be proven by

9 Criminal Code of Canada, Article 319(3)(b).

10 Anti-Discrimination Act 1977 (No. 48) [New South Wales], Section 49ZT(2)(c) (emphasis added). See also Section 38S(2)(c).

11 High Court of The Hague, *el-Moumni*, Case No. 2200359302, Judgment of 18 November 2002.

12 Criminal Code of the Netherlands, resp. Articles 137c and 137d.

the prosecution, in relation to the former count the local Court of Rotterdam held that, yes, in a TV interview he had committed this offence by considering homosexuality harmful for Dutch society and by referring to this sexual orientation as a disease; however, the Court next held that according to established jurisprudence by the Dutch Supreme Court[13] the criminal nature of such a speech act is pardoned 'if the messages directly express a religious opinion'.[14] Having consulted an Islam expert, the Court held that el-Moumni could genuinely base his religious views on the Koran and sayings of the Prophet.[15] The Court concluded that 'protection against prosecution is rendered by the constitutionally protected right to freedom of religion and religious practice'.[16] The judgment was upheld by a Dutch High Court.[17] It should be reiterated, though, that the emerging 'scripture defence'[18] here exclusively applied to the more specific (and low threshold) crime of publicly insulting homosexuals, not to high threshold incitement offences. Indeed, arguably both the criminal law approach used (public insult) and the solution found (a principled scripture defence) are flawed. The former for placing the threshold for interference with free (religious) speech much too low, tremendously lower in any event than under an incitement offence; the latter for carving out a defence apparently quite independent from the (potential) effects, harms and risks emanating from the speech act. That is to say, an anti-incitement approach would likely have yielded the same outcome, but based on a fundamentally different prosecutorial and judicial reasoning: While the religious nature of el-Moumni did not render his speech immune from judicial scrutiny, the offensive nature of his intervention arguably did not engage the threshold of incitement to discrimination or violence.

---

13 Viz., Hoge Raad, *Van Dijke*, Case No. 00945/99, Judgment of 9 January 2001, concerning a Dutch (Christian) politician who was acquitted of publicly insulting homosexuals on the grounds that he had biblically motivated his offensive statements made in an interview with a Dutch periodical.

14 Court of Rotterdam, *el-Moumni*, Case No. 10/040070-01, Judgment of 8 April 2002 (transl. author; original reads as follows: '*wanneer die uitlatingen een godsdienstige overtuiging direct uitdrukken*').

15 *Ibid.*

16 *Ibid.* (transl. author).

17 High Court of The Hague, *el-Moumni*, Case No. 2200359302, Judgment of 18 November 2002.

18 See also High Court of Arnhem, Case No. 21-000117-00, Judgment of 26 June 2001, confirming a lower court acquittal of a pastor who had deemed homosexuality sinful in his letter to the editor of a local newspaper. Again the fact that the impugned statements were embedded within references to the bible removed the criminal nature of the accused's speech act.

The Swedish *Åke Green* case revolves around a Pentecostal Christian pastor.[19] Pastor Green gave a sermon entitled 'Is homosexuality congenital or the powers of evil meddling with people' to some 50 persons. In this sermon, Green started off questioning the legalization of same-sex partnerships, which would cause 'unparalleled catastrophes'. Subsequently, in the course of the sermon a cocktail of quintessential homophobic views are presented: homosexuality as the cause of AIDS; conflation of homosexuality and paedophilia; homosexuality as disease; homosexuality – immediately contradicting the previous point – as but a life-style, a whimsical choice, and so on; all more or less embedded within his biblical understanding of homosexuality as a sin, including the odd biblical reference. Convicted of 'agitation' against homosexuals at a previous instance, the Supreme Court of Sweden ultimately acquits him.

This agitation offence, it may be recalled, was also central to the later European Court of Human Rights case of *Vejdeland*. Indeed, in that latter case the Government of Sweden argued before the Strasbourg Court that the two cases ought to be firmly distinguished since unlike the flyering homophobic neo-Nazis in *Vejdeland*, Green is 'a pastor [who] made his statements before his congregation in a sermon based on certain biblical quotations'.[20]

In coming to its conclusions in the *Green* case the Swedish Supreme Court places tremendous emphasis on the religious nature of the person of the accused and his statements. That said, a principled and comprehensive 'sermon exception' to incitement (here: 'agitation') was not accepted. Indeed, the Supreme Court reiterates the drafting history of the offence and recalls that the Swedish Council of Free Churches had lobbied for such a legal exception, but the Government had ultimately rejected it.[21] For one thing, such was the Government's response, the incitement law would make it in any event sufficiently clear that 'free and objective debate' was not restricted and the purpose of the law was not 'to prevent reasoning and discussion on homosexuality, bisexuality or heterosexuality either in churches or elsewhere in the community. It must also be possible for homosexuals and others, in a free and open debate, to answer and correct erroneous conceptions and in

19 Supreme Court of Sweden, *Prosecutor General v. Åke Green*, Case No. B1050-05, Judgment of 29 November 2005. For an analysis, including the transnational context and the lobbies on both sides of the debate, see Clifford Bob, 'The Global Battle over Religious Expression: Sweden's Åke Green Case in Local and Transnational Perspective', 40:2 *Journal of Ethnic and Migration Studies* (2014), pp. 212–229.

20 European Court of Human Rights, *Vejdeland and Others v. Sweden*, Application No. 1813/07, Judgment of 9 February 2012, para. 15.

21 Supreme Court of Sweden, *Åke Green*, at pp. 5–7.

that way counteract prejudices that would otherwise be at risk of being preserved and perpetuated in concealment'.[22] A similar intervention was made by the Constitutional Standing Committee during the parliamentary (*Riksdag*) considerations of the incitement legislation. While it held on the one hand that '[a]s regards sermon situations, it would *probably*, in the opinion of the Standing Committee, *normally* fall outside the criminal area to quote religious sources and only exhort the hearers to follow the direction of the sources',[23] on the other hand it insisted:

> with reference to a motion [which proposed a sermon-exception], that it is not the intention for separate rules to apply to statements made for example in a sermon situation, compared with spreading the same statements in some other context. The Standing Committee shared the assessment made by the Chancellor of Justice in a statement to the Standing Committee that there can be no question of giving overall special treatment for example to what in the motion are declared to be statements that are in the nature of prescriptive or normative.[24]

Accordingly, as far as the law's *travaux préparatoires* are concerned, the incitement rules do apply to sermon settings in principle. The Swedish Supreme Court, however, moves on to carve out a limited religious freedom defence after all. Based on a legal comparison of Swedish incitement law with the jurisprudence of the European Court of Human Rights, more specifically a combined Article 9 and 10 ECHR analysis (i.e. freedom of religion and expression), the Swedish Supreme Court concludes that the Strasbourg Court does render special protection to speech acts by religious leaders and within sermon-like settings. Emphasizing then once again that pastor Green 'made his statements in a sermon before his congregation on a theme that is in the Bible', it would be likely that placing limits on Green's 'right to preach his biblically-based opinion' would amount to a violation of the Convention.[25]

In sum, while a categorical sermon exception is rejected, the Swedish Supreme Court all but carves out a 'scripture defence'.[26] Strikingly, the Court

22 Supreme Court of Sweden citing from Govt. Bill 2001/02:59, *ibid.* at p. 41 *et seq.*

23 The emphasized words obviously amount to important caveats in their own right.

24 Supreme Court of Sweden paraphrasing, at p. 7, Standing Committee Report 2001/02:KU23, p. 36 *et seq.*

25 Supreme Court of Sweden, *Åke Green*, at p. 16.

26 In this section the Supreme Court furthermore reasons that the Swedish legislator had settled on too low a threshold when it inserted the word 'contempt' into the law.

quite literally expresses a fear of being reproached by the European Court of Human Rights in the event of a hate speech ('agitation') conviction, while Sweden's obligations under international law to combat incitement to discrimination are ignored.[27]

Other judicial instances show (more or less) explicit rejections of a (categorical) religious freedom defence. The clearest example perhaps is the British case of *Hammond v. DPP*.[28] The case in first instance revolved around a street preacher who showcased in public 'a large double sided sign made bearing the words: "Stop Immorality", "Stop Homosexuality" and "Stop Lesbianism" on each side and attached to a pole', but also containing in each of the sign's corners the words 'Jesus is Lord'.[29] Hammond was convicted under the Public Order Act 1986, which prohibits 'threatening, abusive or insulting words or behaviour, or disorderly behaviour or to display any writing, sign or other visible representation which is threatening, abusive or insulting within the hearing or sight of a person likely to be caused harassment, alarm or distress thereby'.[30] Upon appeal the question was extensively discussed whether the act of displaying this sign should be deemed covered by the preacher's combined freedoms of religion and expression, as also enshrined in Articles 9 and 10 of the European Convention on Human Rights. Lord Justice May, writing for the Divisional Court, rejected an outright religious freedom defence,[31] while endorsing a previous instance's ruling that these fundamental rights indeed applied to Mr. Hammond but were legitimately restricted when he was convicted under the Public Order Act.[32]

Quite in the face of the previously outlined Canadian criminal law-enshrined religious freedom defence to hate speech charges,[33] in a case before the Canadian Supreme Court concerning anti-gay flyers,[34] this Court rejected

27 It will be argued in this chapter (*infra*) that the Supreme Court arguably comes to the correct final judgment yet more convincing paths thereto were available.

28 Divisional Court, *Hammond v. DPP*, [2004] EWHC 69 (Admin).

29 *Ibid.*, para. 5.

30 Public Order Act 1986, Section 5 (internal sub-paragraph numbers omitted).

31 *Hammond v. DPP*, at paras. 20 and 33.

32 *Ibid.*, at paras. 20-32.

33 Note that the case at hand was reviewed in light of the constitutionality of provincial human rights – including anti-hate speech – legislation; Article 319 of the Criminal Code is only tangentially engaged with once (viz. *Saskatchewan (Human Rights Commission) v. Whatcott*, 2013 SCC 11, [2013] 1 S.C.R. 467, at para. 137). Also, it should be reiterated that this criminal law defence is limited to the category of religious opinions, or beliefs based on religious texts, that are made in 'good faith'.

34 *Saskatchewan (Human Rights Commission) v. Whatcott*, 2013 SCC 11, [2013] 1 S.C.R. 467.

a categorical religious freedom defence. Judge Rothstein on the very issue held that:

> Some interveners [there were an unprecedented 26 third-party interventions in this case] argued that there should be a defence of sincerely held belief. In their view, speech that is made in good faith and on the basis of the speaker's religious beliefs should be given greater protection, or constitute an absolute defence to any prohibition. … [I]f the sincerity of a religious belief would automatically preclude the finding of a contravention of [Canadian hate speech prohibitions], the [Canadian fundamental freedoms'] analysis would be derailed with no balancing of the competing rights. … Apart from that concern, the fact that a person circulates a hate publication in the furtherance of a sincere religious belief goes to the question of the subjective view of the publisher, which is irrelevant to the objective application of the definition of hatred. Allowing the dissemination of hate speech to be excused by a sincerely held belief would, in effect, provide an absolute defence and would gut the prohibition of effectiveness.[35]

An earlier Canadian judgment had in fact come rather close to accepting a scripture defence. In *Hellquist v. Owens* a local court judge had concluded that advertisements placed by Owens which invoked a number of biblical passages, including one (Leviticus 20:13) that holds that it is 'detestable' that a man lie with a man and that those who do so 'must be put to death', were not protected by freedom of expression or freedom of religion as the advertisements had risked exposing homosexuals to hatred, contrary to the regional human rights code.[36] This was, however, overturned upon appeal.[37] The Saskatchewan

---

35 *Ibid.*, paras. 142-143. Further down the judgment Rothstein J. does determine an interference with Mr. Whatcott's ability to disseminate his religious views, an interference which however is subsequently found to be justified in a free and democratic society. *Ibid.*, para. 156 *et seq.*

36 *Hellquist v. Owens*, [2002] 228 SASK. R. 148, 2 (Sask. Q.B.), engaging the criminal hate speech provisions of the Saskatchewan Human Rights Code (S-24.1). A decision initially upheld in *Owens v. Saskatchewan (Human Rights Commission)*, 2002 SKQB 506 (CanLII). See also Richard Moon, *Putting Faith in Hate: When Religion Is the Source or Target of Hate Speech* (Cambridge: Cambridge University Press, 2018), pp. 14–15; and Sarah Stark, 'The Expansion of Canadian Hate Speech Legislation', 10:4 *Law and Business Review of the Americas* (2007), pp. 807–118, at 812–813. For a similar case, see *Saskatchewan (Human Rights Commission) v. Bell*, [1994] 21 C.R.R. (2d) 92, 30 (Sask. App. Ct.).

37 *Owens v. Saskatchewan (Human Rights Commission)*, 2006 SKCA 41.

Court of Appeal, whilst considering that 'the Bible passages referred to by Mr. Owens, or any other sacred text, can serve as a licence for acting unlawfully against gays and lesbians',[38] essentially felt that quoting the bible cannot do a tremendous amount of harm. Remarkably, the Court of Appeal came to that holding on the basis of a comprehensive exegesis of biblical quotes.[39] It first reasons that the bible also contains messages of love and that any objective reader would automatically downplay the cited call for putting homosexuals to death by considering that wider context.[40] Another – equally unconvincing – argument posited by the court is that Owens and his quoted Bible passages incite death in relation to the sin, not the sinner. Death, hence, to homosexual acts, not death to homosexuals. All in all, then, the Court's conclusion is that 'the Bible passages must be seen in a different light than a plain assertion made in contemporary times to the effect that "Homosexuality is evil and homosexuals should be killed" '.[41]

The question really is, why? That plain assertion – i.e. that someone who selects a quote calling for the death of practising homosexuals is supportive of that very call – is rather convincing for all its plainness. True, that call is not sufficient in its own right, when considering international incitement standards, to conclude that the advertisement including the biblical quotes were likely to incite imminent harm to homosexuals. But what the Court does is essentially cut off that additional context-based risk assessment by holding that quoting scripture simply *cannot be* dangerous since objective readers would be able to dismantle the words used. This may well be an underestimation of the

38 *Ibid.*, para 87.

39 *Ibid.*, paras. 79-83.

40 The court's exact words (*ibid.*, para. 79) are: 'the passages cited by Mr. Owens are self-evidently part of a larger work, the Bible, and would tend to be seen as such by an objective observer. One need not be a Biblical scholar, or even a Christian, to know that the Bible as a whole is the source of more than one sort of message and, more specifically, is the source of messages involving themes of love, tolerance and forgiveness. It contains many passages of that sort: Mark 12:31 "Love your neighbor as yourself."; Matthew 6:14-15 "For if you forgive men when they sin against you, your heavenly Father will also forgive you. But if you do not forgive men their sins, your Father will not forgive your sins." Matthew 7:1 "Do not judge, or you too will be judged." Leviticus 19:18 "Do not seek revenge or bear a grudge against one of your people, but love your neighbour as yourself." Proverbs 10:12 "Hatred stirs up dissension, but love covers over all wrongs." Although, as indicated, the Court cannot authoritatively determine the meaning of sacred writings, it is important to recognize that an objective reader of Mr. Owens' advertisement would see it in the context of the other concepts popularly understood as flowing from the Bible. This would tend to colour the advertisement as something falling below [the applicable hate speech standard]'.

41 *Ibid.*, para. 83.

impugned content, and an overestimation of readers. Again, the likelihood of harm could arguably have been challenged in this case for a number of reasons to do with the context of the speech act, but to deem the content (and intent) of the speech act free from incitement purely because a religious source is quoted amounts to a questionable content and intent assessment.

Naturally, the assessment whether an impugned speech amounted to punishable incitement may hinge strongly on the content of the speech act in question, not because it is a quote from scripture but because it is clear that the speech act was not extreme enough to meet the content-threshold of incitement. Such was the case in another Canadian case, *Lund v. Boissoin*, according to the Alberta Court of Appeal.[42] Whereas the Alberta Human Rights Panel had concluded that a letter to the editor drafted by a Christian pastor in which he, Boissoin, deemed homosexuality wicked and sinful and held that its acceptance should not be taught to children, ran counter to the hate speech provision,[43] the Court of Appeal overruled this on the grounds that the impugned speech act was not grave enough and was hence exempt from the hate speech prohibition and fully covered by freedom of expression and religion. The judgment emphasizes that the hate speech provision in question 'provides no exemption for religious leaders or public places of worship'.[44] The judgment concludes that the letter may be bigoted and insulting,[45] but it falls outside the ambit of the – problematically formulated[46] – applicable extreme speech provision.

---

42 *Lund v. Boissoin*, 2012 ABCA 300 (CanLII). See also Moon, *supra* note 36, p. 15, for an analysis of this case.

43 *Viz.*, Human Rights, Multiculturalism and Citizenship Act, RSA 2000, c H-14 (Act), section 3.

44 *Lund v. Boissoin*, para. 76.

45 *Ibid.*, para. 71: 'the letter is essentially an expression of Boissoin's opinion that teaching children at school that homosexuality is normal, and that same sex families are equivalent to heterosexual families, is morally wrong and should not be tolerated. In the words of the panel, the "letter is, on the face of it, a critique of the homosexual agenda which [Boissoin] alleged existed in the school system in Red Deer, Alberta" ... Boissoin hoped to rouse others of like mind and involve them in the public debate. While his views are expressed in strong, insensitive, and some might say bigoted terms, the words are clearly the expression of his opinion. And the aim of the letter was to stir apathetic people, who agreed with him, to his cause'.

46 *Ibid.*, paras. 95-96: 'The goals of protecting the freedoms of expression and religion, on the one hand, and protecting vulnerable minorities from discrimination, on the other, are matters of primary concern to the citizens of this Province. It is unfortunate, therefore, that [the hate speech provision] gives rise to the difficulties of interpretation manifest in this judgment and the decisions below. This lack of clarity has resulted in this protracted litigation, to the detriment and expense of all parties. The Attorney General in his factum

A sweeping religious freedom defence was also rejected by the South African High Court in a case concerning an ordained minister.[47] The respondent's various published homophobic remarks resulted in a 30-day prison sentence. Judge Bozalek, writing for the majority, also took into account that he had committed similar crimes of inciting hatred and harm against homosexuals before – indeed, the judgment at hand is in essence a contempt of court case. Through various speech acts, including online articles and reactions posted underneath online articles by others, Mr. Bougaardt compared homosexuals to paedophiles, called them perverted and 'animals' who ought to be locked up in cages.[48] At one time he invited, through one of his online posts, ISIS to 'rid' South Africa of the 'homosexual curse'.

One of the defences at his trial was that he enjoys the constitutional right to freedom of expression and particularly the freedom to pronounce his religious beliefs.[49] The High Court rejects this defence.[50] However, not unlike the Swedish *Green* case a more limited 'biblical defence' is considered by the court. Indeed, the High Court observes that earlier charges of homophobic hate speech which had led to Bougaardt being interdicted were in fact settled (with the Human Rights Commission) out of court, obliging him not to repeat acts of homophobic incitement whilst at the same time protecting his right to 'preach the word of God and what the Bible directs'.[51] Yet this exception does not amount to a full-fledged religious freedom defence and the High Court concludes, moreover, that he went rather beyond the limits of such a limited scripture defence:

> [n]o attempt was made in these proceedings, and correctly so, to justify the statements made by the respondent on biblical or religious grounds. The respondent has a right to freedom of speech and to his religious beliefs and to express these but none of the statements made by him

claims the ability to limit expression that is characterized as "hateful" or "contemptuous" only when such expression "is linked to acts of discrimination falling within provincial subject matters". In his view, section 3 is to be interpreted as "dealing with a narrow range of extreme expression that clearly falls outside the bounds of normal discourse *and leads to discriminatory acts*" ... If that is the intent of the legislators, it would be helpful if they said so clearly' (paragraph numbers omitted from the quote).

47 High Court of South Africa (Western Cape Division, Cape Town), *South African Human Rights Commission v. Oscar Peter Bougaardt*, Case No. EC13/2013, Judgment of 18 May 2018.

48 *Ibid.*, paras. 7-15.

49 *Ibid.*, para. 27.

50 *Ibid.*, para. 29.

51 For the full settlement, see *ibid.*, para. 4.

> which are the subject of these proceedings[s] fall within those parameters. In short they dehumanise and demonise gay and lesbian persons and, without a shred of proof, make wide and damaging assertions that members of such community engage in criminal or anti-social conduct.[52]

Accordingly, the judgment (i) rejects an outright religious freedom defence against homophobic hate speech charges; (ii) while contemplating and endorsing a religious scripture defence; and (iii) at the same time insisting that any such defence may not be invoked unjustifiably.

The latter aspect is significant, since it implies that this defence, if invoked, comes with a burden of proof to substantiate that scripture, and nothing but scripture, motivated the speech acts. Also, the fact that the judgment in this particular case second-guesses a church minister's reading of the scope of scripture suggests that judicial oversight can be exercised. The judge's role here certainly is a most delicate one: While a secular judge cannot unduly encroach on religious autonomy and certainly cannot assume any ecclesiastical authority, justice may still require an enquiry into the question whether the hateful speech act can be premised on scripture or whether human agency functioned as a punishable additional intermediary between scripture per se and the hateful speech act. That is, whether more was said than scripture per se and whether these additions engage criminal law, thus engaging criminal liability beyond the margins of the applicable defence.

It is tempting to adopt a no-nonsense approach here and argue that surely secular judges can make this call, are perfectly able to sift through bona fide invocations of religious sources and distinguish those from claims not made in good faith. And even if they are not always capable to do so themselves, expert testimony can be solicited in court to help out and establish definitively what scripture does and does not say.

And yet, the above cases and underlying laws or judicial approaches unveil the downsides of a priori (partial) legal defences and the a priori balances between free religious speech and equal dignity rights that flow from such defences. Such legal defences premise the calibration act far too heavily on the intent test and on the question whether the speaker was permitted to opine the impugned message in the light of religious doctrine. International incitement prohibitions require a far more objective context-based risk assessment, an assessment wherein intentions are part of the puzzle but not decisive and an assessment not wholly dependent on the answer to the question if what

52 *Ibid.*, para. 29.

was said can be based on scripture or not.[53] Decisive is whether what was said could, in the circumstances of the case, be interpreted as an act of incitement and, moreover, be deemed likely to cause imminent acts of discrimination or violence.

None of this means that the overall religious context in which the statements were made is immaterial. To be sure, international human rights law contains mandatory prohibitions of advocacy of religious hatred, but that does not mean that a speech act's religious context is inconsequential. Furthermore, international human rights law renders strong protection to religious freedom,[54] but at the same time it must be observed that this right is not an absolute one and that the right is not only subject to its general restriction grounds (protecting rights of others and such public goods as public order), but is also subject to such limitations as may flow in particular contexts from incitement prohibitions and the general 'abuse of rights' doctrine. The latter clauses provide that no one may use their rights with a view towards destroying the rights of others and can be found in all major civil and political rights treaties, including the ICCPR and the ECHR.[55] In the present context this means that religious freedom cannot be invoked with the sole purpose of seeking to destroy the equal dignity rights of others.

International human rights law finds fault with any *a priori* balancing of rights whether by immunizing certain speech settings or certain speech content or by, conversely, deeming the religious nature of speech settings and content altogether immaterial. Context is crucial and the question as to whether

53 See also Moon, *supra* note 36, Ch. 5 (esp. p. 136), arguing that the very notion that scripture as an exclusive isolated motivation is problematic in se when scriptural and hence religious prohibitions are involved. Religious prohibitions focus on behaviour and assume behaviour is a choice and call upon the flock to resist the evils of certain behaviours-as-choices.

54 ICCPR, Article 18. This Covenant's freedom of religion or belief clause provides in full: '1. Everyone shall have the right to freedom of thought, conscience and religion. This right shall include freedom to have or to adopt a religion or belief of his choice, and freedom, either individually or in community with others and in public or private, to manifest his religion or belief in worship, observance, practice and teaching. 2. No one shall be subject to coercion which would impair his freedom to have or to adopt a religion or belief of his choice. 3. Freedom to manifest one's religion or beliefs may be subject only to such limitations as are prescribed by law and are necessary to protect public safety, order, health, or morals or the fundamental rights and freedoms of others. 4. The States Parties to the present Covenant undertake to have respect for the liberty of parents and, when applicable, legal guardians to ensure the religious and moral education of their children in conformity with their own convictions'. See also ECHR, Article 9.

55 Resp. ICCPR, Article 5(1); ECHR, Article 17.

we are dealing with religious discourse is one such factor that fills in the circumstances of the case and hence this factor – among other important context factors – fosters the necessary case-by-case analysis determining whether the speech act amounted to protected speech or punishable incitement.[56]

3 The Theory of Context

Recent international benchmarks and conceptualizations offered by monitoring bodies and independent experts offer comparable insights. These benchmarks include first and foremost the *Rabat Plan of Action on the prohibition of advocacy of national, racial or religious hatred that constitutes incitement to discrimination, hostility or violence*;[57] the UN Human Rights Committee's *General Comment No. 34* on freedom of expression (dedicating its closing paragraphs to incitement);[58] the Committee on the Elimination of Racial Discrimination' *General Recommendation No. 35* on combating racist hate speech;[59] the UN Special Rapporteur on freedom of religion or belief's 2013 thematic report on manifestations of collective religious hatred;[60] and the Special Rapporteur on freedom of expression's 2012 report on hate speech and incitement.[61] While the *Rabat Plan* was heavily influenced by ARTICLE 19's conceptual work on

56 On judging incitement and the role of context, see Jeroen Temperman, *Religious Hatred and International Law: The Prohibition of Incitement to Violence or Discrimination* (Cambridge: Cambridge University Press, 2016), Chapter 10 ('The Context of Religious Hatred').

57 *Rabat Plan of Action on the prohibition of advocacy of national, racial or religious hatred that constitutes incitement to discrimination, hostility or violence*, Conclusions and recommendations emanating from the four regional expert workshops organised by OHCHR in 2011, adopted by experts in Rabat, Morocco on 5 October 2012 (hereafter also 'Rabat Plan of Action') and endorsed by the UN OHCHR, *Report of the United Nations High Commissioner for Human Rights on the expert workshops on the prohibition of incitement to national, racial or religious hatred* (A/HRC/22/17/Add.4, 2013). This plan is in turn strongly inspired by ARTICLE 19, *Prohibiting Incitement to Discrimination, Hostility or Violence: Policy Brief* (2012).

58 Human Rights Committee, *General Comment No. 34: Article 19: Freedoms of Opinion and Expression*, CCPR/C/GC/34 (2011), particularly paras. 50-52.

59 Committee on the Elimination of Racial Discrimination, *General Recommendation 35: Combating Racist Hate Speech*, CERD/C/GC/35 (2013).

60 Special Rapporteur on Freedom of Religion or Belief, *Tackling Manifestations of Collective Religious Hatred*, A/HRC/25/58 (2013).

61 Special Rapporteur on the Promotion and Protection of the Right to Freedom of Opinion and Expression, *Report of the Special Rapporteur to the General Assembly on Hate Speech and Incitement to Hatred*, A/67/357 (2012).

incitement, most of the subsequent expert reports, in turn, expressly reference and endorse the principles and benchmarks set out in the *Rabat Plan*, thus firmly entrenching these benchmarks in the authoritative workings of international monitoring bodies and independent experts.[62]

Incitement, as an international law notion, has also been subject to more intense legal scholarship in recent times. There, incitement (unlike for instance 'insult' or 'provocation' offences) is conceptualized as a *triangular* offense.[63] Article 20, paragraph 2, of the ICCPR provides that advocacy of national, racial or religious hatred *that constitutes* incitement to discrimination, hostility or violence is to be prohibited by law. That formulation is premised on the notion that there are hateful speech acts that do, and hateful speech act that do *not*, amount to incitement. Accordingly, what is to be prohibited by State parties is not hateful propaganda as such. Article 20(2) ICCPR does not aim at banning all forms of 'hate speech'. Only those hateful speech acts that 'constitute incitement' to certain adverse acts (discrimination, hostility or violence) are to be prohibited. What this means, in turn, is that incitement is premised on a triangular relationship. An act of incitement requires three parties: an 'inciter', an 'audience', and a 'target group'. Accordingly, the phenomenon of 'incitement' is concerned with various relations:

- those between the *inciter and its audience*: is the former inciting the latter to adverse acts?;
- those between the *inciter and its target group*: is the former saying hateful things about the latter, e.g. dehumanizing them, using stereotypes, or otherwise undermining their humanity or equality?;
- and, crucially, those between the *audience and the target group*: how likely is it that the former, upon having listened to, read or otherwise received the hateful speech act, will be effectively mobilized to carry out

62 Note that the Special Rapporteur on freedom of expression's report also cites ARTICLE 19's work directly, while the Human Rights Committee's General Comment predates the Rabat Plan.

63 See Jeroen Temperman, *Religious Hatred and International Law: The Prohibition of Incitement to Violence or Discrimination* (Cambridge: Cambridge University Press, 2016), esp. chapter 7.3 ('The triangle of incitement'). See also e.g. Agnes Callamard, 'Religion, Terrorism and Speech in a "Post-Charlie Hebdo" World', 10 *Religion & Human Rights: An International Journal* (2015), pp. 207–228, at p. 225 (referencing Temperman's triangle); and, more generally, Peter Molnar, 'Responding to "Hate Speech" with Art, Education, and the Imminent Danger Test', in Michael Herz and Peter Molnar (eds.), *The Content and Context of Hate Speech: Rethinking Regulation and Responses* (Cambridge: Cambridge University Press, 2012), pp. 183–197, at 196, arguing that 'hate speech' is the wrong term and that the focus ought to be on incitement and the harm (violence) that can flow from it at the hands of third parties.

harmful acts, in the form of discrimination, hostility or violence, vis-à-vis the latter?

Accordingly, the offence of incitement is strongly dependent on numerous contextual factors. The actual content of the impugned speech act is only partly useful in order to make the assessment whether a certain speech act amounted to incitement within the meaning of Article 20(2) ICCPR. And since content per se cannot tell the whole story, *content-based legal defences* are problematic. A rule providing that context *x* can never be deemed incitement since content *x* is based on scripture is a problematic rule since international law benchmarks provide that judging incitement depends on so much more than content per se.

The content of the speech act may tell us something about the degree of hatred expressed vis-à-vis a target group. Also, occasionally the intention of the author or speaker may be distilled from the content of the speech or publication. What we often cannot distil from the speech act alone is how likely it is that an audience will indeed become violent, that is, will actually commit violent acts against the target group, or will discriminate against the latter as a result of the speech act. In order to establish such 'likelihood' we need to know more. We need to know the status and role of the speaker. We need to know the position of the target group: how vulnerable is the verbally attacked group? We may need to know how far the speech may reach. And so on.

The *Rabat Plan of Action* elaborates on *content* per se as follows:

> The content of the speech constitutes one of the key foci of the court's deliberations and is a critical element of incitement. Content analysis may include the degree to which the speech was provocative and direct, as well as a focus on the form, style, nature of the arguments deployed in the speech at issue or in the balance struck between arguments deployed ...[64]

The five additional factors, together filling in the speech act's context, are:

- *context;*
- *intent;*
- *speaker;*
- *extent;* and
- *likelihood, including imminence.*[65]

64 Rabat Plan of Action, para. 22 (A/HRC/22/17/Add.4, para. 29).

65 Rabat Plan of Action, para. 22 (A/HRC/22/17/Add.4, para. 29).

Thus, indeed, somewhat confusingly one of the context factors is 'context', perhaps best referred to as *overall context*, that is, the wider socio-political and historical context in which the hateful statement is made. The Rabat Plan defines overall context as follows:

> Context is of great importance when assessing whether particular statements are likely to incite to discrimination, hostility or violence against the target group and it may have a bearing directly on both intent and/or causation. Analysis of the context should place the speech act within the social and political context prevalent at the time the speech was made and disseminated.[66]

Accordingly, 'context' may shed more light on other relevant factors. Most important in that regard, an overall context assessment may have a direct bearing on the question of 'likelihood'; that is, the question as to how likely it was that following the hateful speech act harmful acts would be carried out by the audience against the speech's target group.

Next there is the question of intent or *mens rea* in criminal law: what was the mind-set of the inciter at the material time? The Rabat Plan of Action reflects on intent in the following manner:

> Article 20 of the ICCPR requires intent. Negligence and recklessness are not sufficient for an article 20 situation which requires "advocacy" and "incitement" rather than mere distribution or circulation. In this regard, it requires the activation of a triangular relationship between the object and subject of the speech as well as the audience.[67]

Furthermore, aside from the speaker's intention, also the very position, that is, the *speaker's role and/or status* may be pertinent and obviously differs from case to case. The status of the speaker may, after all, have a direct bearing upon the potential impact of their words and hence on the question of likelihood of harm stemming from those words. In the words of the Rabat Plan, '[t]he position or status of the speaker in the society should be considered, specifically the individual's or organisation's standing in the context of the audience to whom the speech is directed'.[68]

---

66 Rabat Plan of Action, para. 22 (A/HRC/22/17/Add.4, para. 29).

67 *Ibid.*

68 *Ibid.*

The Rabat Plan of Action next emphasizes the '*extent*' of the speech, describing this context factor in the following terms:

> This includes elements such as the reach of the speech, its public nature, magnitude and the size of its audience. Further elements are whether the speech is public, what the means of dissemination are, considering whether the speech was disseminated through one single leaflet or through broadcasting in the mainstream media or internet, what was the frequency, the amount and the extent of the communications, whether the audience had the means to act on the incitement, whether the statement (or work of art) was circulated in a restricted environment or widely accessible to the general public.[69]

The 'extent' or 'reach' of the speech and the medium used directly impact the question of how likely it is that the target group will face violence or discrimination from the speech act's audience.[70] The actual context in a concrete case, including for instance the relatively minimal 'extent' of the speech, could hence also very well be that such that risks are quite minimal.

The Rabat Plan of Action, finally, lists the question of '*likelihood*' as a paramount factor. This factor includes the question whether the target group is hitherto well respected or rather, whether it for instance suffers from ongoing (societal) persecution. Statistics on hate crimes should, for instance, be taken into account in that respect. Implying this is the most crucial context factor, the *Rabat Plan* states that

> [i]ncitement, by definition, is an inchoate crime. The action advocated through incitement speech does not have to be committed for that speech to amount to a crime. Nevertheless some degree of risk of resulting harm must be identified. It means the courts will have to determine that there was a reasonable probability that the speech would succeed in inciting actual action against the target group, recognising that such causation should be rather direct.[71]

---

69 *Ibid.*

70 The question of online hatred and its border-crossing impact is a complicating factor and beyond the focus of the present contribution; for a detailed study, see Tarlach McGonagle, *The Council of Europe against Online Hate Speech: Conundrums and Challenges* (Council of Europe expert paper, MCM(2013)005, 2013).

71 Rabat Plan of Action, para. 22 (A/HRC/22/17/Add.4, para. 29).

This emphasis on the *inchoate* nature of the crime of incitement is important. While the 'likelihood' factor forces a risk assessment, causality is by no means required. Indeed, save in the area of judging the risks of announced demonstrations or publications, typically the relevant legal assessment occurs ex post. The fact that, after the speech act, no acts of violence or discrimination ensued at the hands of a third-party audience is essentially immaterial. A hate speaker's criminal liability should be assessed on the basis of the speech and the risks it posed to the rights of others at the material time, i.e. when the speech act first became a public one. The reverse situation (third-party violence and discrimination closely following a speech act), however, can obviously be appreciated as tell-tale signs as to the likelihood of harm, but again are not decisive in light of the inchoate nature of the crime. That is to say, in that scenario too content and intent must be duly investigated.

According to the Rabat Plan of Action, the question of likelihood must include a reflection on the '*imminence*' of harmful acts flowing from a hateful speech act. In other words, it is not enough that harm is 'likely' sometime in the future – at the material time, that is, right after a hateful speech has been published or otherwise made public, such harm must be 'imminent'. Imminence is not so much an additional and independent factor, the Rabat Plan of Action rather deems it an integral quality of the type of likelihood required under this content-intent-context assessment test.

4 The Application of Context

Domestic law and case law show varying levels of 'responsiveness' to such comprehensive context-based risk assessment as is emerging under international benchmarks. Applying such a comprehensive context test may – even though at times unfair[72] – be helpful in illustrating stronger and weaker aspects of judicial reasoning.

Naturally, those decisions that accept a sweeping religious freedom defence immediately fail the context test. The fact that a speech act amounts to religious discourse does not mean the same speech act cannot also amount to an act of hateful incitement within the meaning of international law. Even a strict scripture recital could, depending on the other context factors (intent, speaker, extent, likelihood, etc.), amount to incitement. The bridge between

72 Because executed with the benefit of hindsight and so occasionally very much retroactively, on the basis of newly emerging international benchmarks.

historical intolerant texts and contemporary acts of incitement is human agency. A scripture defence (as contemplated or even accepted in such cases as the Swedish *Green* case or the South African *Bougaardt* case) cuts off the necessary legal assessment prematurely. The fact that the alleged inciter merely or mostly quoted directly from scripture certainly helps placing the case in perspective. Yet, assessing the gravity of a case may require posing and addressing additional context questions, such as questions in relation to intent, speaker, extent, and likelihood.

That said, it may of course be that a concrete instance of homophobic speech plain and simply is not severe enough to engage the applicable extreme speech restrictions. For instance, in a French case an earlier conviction of a French politician was reversed out of concern with the necessity of that conviction.[73] The accused, Christian X, had stated among other things that homosexuality is 'inferior' to heterosexuality, his argument being that, unlike the latter sexual orientation, when the former would become the universal standard there would be a 'danger to humanity'. The Court of Cassation deconstructs that statement and analyses it extensively in the light of (international) free speech protection and ultimately rules that, though doubtless insensitive and insulting, this speech act does not incite violence or otherwise amounts to punishable speech. While distasteful, it is indeed questionable – in nearly any context – whether a speech act like this is likely to mobilize people against homosexuals to commit acts of discrimination or violence against them. While not all-decisive, content itself does directly impact the question of likelihood; here the relatively benign content puts into question the likelihood of imminent harm. Put differently, it would require an exceptional context defined by extreme vulnerability on the part of homosexuals, for this speech act to function as fuel to fire. None of that was applicable in this case.

A recent British case similarly turned on the question of severity of the homophobic speech acts.[74] Whereas the removal of Felix Ngole from his Master's programme in Social Work over his online homophobic behaviour – among other things calling homosexuality sinful and illustrating his views with biblical quotations[75] – was sanctioned in an earlier judicial instance, the Court of Appeals held among other things that '[t]he mere expression of views on theological grounds (e.g. that "homosexuality is a sin") does not necessarily connote that the person expressing such views will discriminate on such

73 Cour de Cassation, *Christian X*, Case No. 07-83398, judgment of 12 November 2008.

74 Court of Appeal, *R. (Ngole) v. University of Sheffield*, [2019] EWCA Civ 1127, Judgment of 3 July 2019.

75 *Ibid.*, paras. 10-11.

grounds. In the present case, there was positive evidence to suggest that the Appellant had never discriminated on such grounds in the past and was not likely to do so in the future (because, as he explained, the Bible prohibited him from discriminating against anybody)'.[76] This being a civil and not a criminal law case, the questions of intent and gravity here related not so much to the risk of third persons following his homophobic sentiments, but rather whether his expressed views made him unfit for (pursuing) social work. The Court of Appeals overturned his removal from his studies as the University of Sheffield had not sufficiently substantiated why his fitness to practice was irredeemably impaired; neither was it made clear that the removal was the best way to address any concerns in that regard.[77] Considering the fact that no warning was given, the court held that the sanction was disproportionate.[78]

By contrast, if the gravity of the homophobic speech act is serious, yet questions remain in that department, it may very well be context factors that function as the proverbial straw to tip the balance in favour of a finding of incitement. In a Dutch case concerning a homophobic politician 'context' proves all-decisive to his ultimate conviction.[79] In an earlier instance, before the High Court of Amsterdam, the local Amsterdam politician Delano Felter was acquitted. This judgment went on to be quashed by the Dutch Supreme Court, indicating that in cases of homophobic speech special 'attention must be paid to the exact wording of the statement as well as the context in which the latter was done'.[80] In that regard, the Supreme Court found that the High Court had focussed too much on the question whether this politician had literally incited violence or discrimination against homosexuals and not enough on the question whether the entire context of the impugned statement was not one that amounted to 'incitement to intolerance' against homosexuals, which according to the Supreme Court should be read into the relevant incitement provisions since incitement of intolerance can be regarded as an extension of *incitement to discrimination*.[81] Thus instructed, upon retrial by the Amsterdam High Court, Felter was convicted for inciting discrimination against homosexuals.[82]

76 *Ibid.*, para. 5(10).

77 *Ibid.*, para. 5(6).

78 *Ibid.*, para. 5(12).

79 Hoge Raad, *Felter*, Case No. 13/01327, Judgment of 16 December 2014.

80 *Ibid.*, para. 4.4.3. The judicial tests for determining incitement against homosexuals as established in *Felter* have been confirmed by the Supreme Court in later judgments, for instance in a case concerning a rap artists who used homophobic language in one of his songs: Hoge Raad, *Ismo*, Case No. 17/01485, Judgment of 26 June 2018.

81 *Felter*, para. 4.4.4.

82 Gerechtshof Amsterdam, *Felter*, Case No. 23-004790-14, Judgment of 1 February 2016.

This time round, a comprehensive content-intent-context assessment underpins the verdict's reasoning. The impugned remarks, consisting of some two dozen homophobic statements, were made both during a local election debate and, directly afterwards, during an interview with a local TV station, which, however, broadcasted some of the footage at a later moment in time. The content analysis of the Court points to such fighting words as the repeated expressions that 'they [homosexuals] must go', 'they need to be combated' and 'they must be thrown out' and concludes there can be no doubt that such statements are inciting.[83] In the words of the High Court, '[t]he statements made by the accused incited the audience to discriminate homosexuals by way of tackling them, fighting them and making their life – in the Netherlands or at least in Amsterdam – difficult'.[84] Furthermore, the High Court establishes Felter's criminal intent[85] and extensively discusses the question of the value of public contributions by politicians versus the need of the state to protect homosexuals against inciting statements.[86] By way of risk assessment, the vulnerability of homosexuals as a group in society and as ongoing subject of heated debates is extensively separately considered by the court.[87] While still more concrete risk assessment considerations were imaginable (e.g., to name one issue that comes to the fore: was there a difference in expected impact between the election debate and the televised remarks?; if so it would be in order to dwell on those), this judgment is a good example of an all-round risk assessment required by international human rights standards on incitement and political/religious speech, engaging ample with the combination of content, intent and miscellaneous context factors.

Reassessing relevant case law in the light of a robust context-based risk assessment, concerns about free religious speech should occasionally also be raised. That is, while a categorical religious freedom defence does not sit well with international incitement prohibitions and a legal or judicial rejection thereof is hence fine in principle, such should naturally not lead to insensitiveness as to the importance of protecting religious speech discourse. Religious speech must be protected, unless the speech act qualifies as prohibited incitement or otherwise interferes with the rights of others and a state may under the circumstances of the case legitimately prioritize the competing rights at stake. The case of *Hammond v. DPP*[88] arguably falls into the category of lowering the

83 *Ibid.*, section '*Bewoordingen uitlatingen*'.
84 *Ibid.* (author's translation).
85 *Ibid.*, sections '*Andere context gerelateerde aspecten*' and '*Gevolgtrekking*'.
86 *Ibid.*, esp. in section '*Strafbaarheid van het bewezen verklaarde*'.
87 *Ibid.*
88 The facts of which were outlined *supra*, in the previous section on scripture defences.

protection to intolerant religious speech discourse for the wrong reasons or based on the wrong test. Thus whereas Lord Justice May is right in rejecting a principled religious freedom defence, the ultimate conclusion that an extreme speech conviction (as per the Public Order Act) was warranted is reached in too abrupt a fashion.[89] Lip-service is paid in the concluding part of the judgment to the importance of religious freedom and free religious speech,[90] while there is little reasoning in the way of substantiating the precise dangers that emanated from this street preacher's speech (who, incidentally, mostly got himself into trouble[91]).

In the meantime, British incitement legislation does set the bar relatively high by insisting, in sharp contrast to racist hate speech, that for sexual orientation-based hate speech to be punishable the words must be 'threatening', not just 'abusive' or 'insulting'.[92] Just as merely criticizing, or even ridiculing or insulting religions (i.e. the 'saving clause'),[93] is not covered by the hate speech legislation, speech critical of certain sexual orientations also does not engage the law. Concretely, this means that for instance speech acts containing religiously-motivated normative statements against non-heterosexual orientations or specifically religion-based critiques of same-sex marriage do not as such come within the ambit of speech prohibitions.[94]

89 *Hammond v. DPP*, para. 33-34.

90 For a comprehensive critique of this judgment, see Ian Leigh, 'Hatred, Sexual Orientation Free Speech and Religious Liberty', 10 *Ecclesiastical Law Journal* (2008), at 341–344. See also Ian Leigh, 'Homophobic Speech, Equality Denial, and Religious Expression', in Ivan Hare and James Weinstein (eds.), *Extreme Speech and Democracy* (Oxford: Oxford University Press, 2010), pp. 375–399.

91 'A group of 30 to 40 people gathered around [Mr. Hammond], arguing and shouting; some people in the crowd were angry, others were aggressive or distressed; some threw soil at the appellant; one person was hit over the head with the placard'. *Hammond v. DPP*, para. 5(f).

92 The same goes for religious hatred. See Part 3A of the Public Order Act 1986, as amended by the Criminal Justice and Immigration Act 2008; cf. Racial and Religious Hatred Act 2006.

93 Criminal Justice and Immigration Act 2008, Article 29J: 'Nothing in this Part shall be read or given effect in a way which prohibits or restricts discussion, criticism or expressions of antipathy, dislike, ridicule, insult or abuse of particular religions or the beliefs or practices of their adherents, or of any other belief system or the beliefs or practices of its adherents, or proselytising or urging adherents of a different religion or belief system to cease practising their religion or belief system'.

94 Criminal Justice and Immigration Act 2008, Article 29JA: '(1) In this Part, for the avoidance of doubt, the discussion or criticism of sexual conduct or practices or the urging of persons to refrain from or modify such conduct or practices shall not be taken of itself to be threatening or intended to stir up hatred. (2) In this Part, for the avoidance of doubt,

Stating one's (religiously-motivated) misgivings about certain types of sexual orientation or stating one's (religiously-motivated) misgivings about same-sex marriage does not in and for itself amount to incitement on grounds of sexual orientation. Richard Moon comes to a similar conclusion, via a different route, namely by looking closer at the content of the speech and by placing this within the perspective of commonness, as opposed to the extremity, of such belief systems. He contends that scripture-based anti-homosexuality speech that

> simply asserts that homosexual practice is sinful (citing the Bible) ... is not sufficiently extreme to count as hate speech. In contrast to religiously grounded racist speech, anti-gay views are still held by a significant number of Christians, Muslims, and others (even if that number is rapidly diminishing), and so such views are not easily dismissed or ignored as "bad" religion.[95]

Matters are different, though, when additional extremity, including incitement, enters the equation:

> Anti-gay speech may amount to hate speech, though, when it calls for the punishment (and, in its most extreme form, the death) of those who breach the Biblical prohibition on homosexuality or when it links homosexuality to paedophilia (a connection that has no specific religious basis), presenting gays as a menace, or, in religious terms, a source of evil and corruption.[96]

By the same logic, non-qualified 'gendercritical' speech does not automatically come within the ambit of transphobic incitement prohibitions. Whether religiously informed or not, the normative position that one believes in biological 'sex' and is critical of the notion of 'gender' is as such covered by the freedom to hold opinions and when expressed publicly, by the freedom of expression.

The defence that is opening up here, at the same time, should not be uncritically accepted by courts. In a recent British case, the self-proclaimed 'transcritical' views on Twitter included fairly outspoken transphobic statements,[97]

---

any discussion or criticism of marriage which concerns the sex of the parties to marriage shall not be taken of itself to be threatening or intended to stir up hatred'.

95 Moon, *supra* note 36, p. 14.

96 *Ibid.*

97 *R. (Miller) v. The College of Policing & The Chief Constable of Humberside*, [2020] EWHC 225 (Admin), judgment of 14 February 2019. See also, Alice Irving, 'Twitter, Trans Rights

but the court was quick, arguably too quick, to accept that the content was not extreme enough to engage speech limitations. Mr Miller had tweeted some 30-odd 'transcritical' messages, including the following: 'I was assigned Mammal at Birth, but my orientation is Fish. Don't mis species me, fuckers'.[98] While offensive, that particular message indeed 'simply' questions transgenderism as a phenomenon; another tweet, however, implicitly trivialized violence against transgenders: 'Is Trans Day of Remembrance a thing, then? Like, an actual one?' Transgender Day of Remembrance, annually observed on 20 November, commemorates transgenders killed through transphobic hate crimes – the global tally increasing each year, totalling 350 killings in 2020. His tweet hence trivializes the value of the lives lost and explicitly deems this annual memorialization some sort of misplaced attention to the plight, security and rights of transgenders. On its face, it may be questionable whether Miller, in so tweeting, glorified transphobic violence, yet that was precisely one of the issues that required separate and elaborate discussion on the merits. The same goes for a number of other specific tweets through which Miller urged men to be more critical of transgenderism ('Any idea why men aren't being more vocally GC [gendercritical] I know there's a few of us, but I expect way more').[99] While it is clear that in Miller's worldview there's no room for acceptance of transgenderism, some of these tweets raise the question whether urging others to be more outspoken and to voice similar intolerance amounted to incitement of discrimination. One of the questions raised by cases like this is whether one can verbally attack transgenderism as a phenomenon without at the same time attacking transgender persons, at the very least by way of trivializing their plight and their legal standing. The court did not pursue any of these matters. Instead the Court rushed to side with Miller, quite uncritically accepting that his views amounted to legitimate debate on a contentious issue (and in between the lines accuses the person who brought the complaint against Mr Miller of hysteria).[100] The context, rightly emphasized by the court, underlying the case involved extreme vulnerability on the part of the targeted group:

> Trans people continue to face significant barriers to full participation in public life. Reported hate crime is rising. Reported self-harm and suicide

---

and the Role of the Police: An Extended Look', UK Human rights Blog (21 February 2020, available at <https://ukhumanrightsblog.com/2020/02/21/twitter-trans-rights-and-the-role-of-the-police-an-extended-look/>).

98 *Ibid.*, para. 42.

99 *Ibid.*, para. 54.

100 *Ibid.*, paras. 262-287.

> rates, particularly amongst young trans people, are extremely concerning. Trans people continue to face discrimination and stigma, in employment and in the provision of public services.[101]

A more focussed assessment as to whether these transphobic messages, disseminated under the cloak of critical discourse, may foster such stigma and discrimination would have been in order.

It is clear, in any event, that there is a particularly fine line here between normative (judgmental) statements on matters of sexual orientation and gender identity and *incitement to discrimination* particularly. 'Hate the sin, love the sinner' may be feasible on paper, practice is a different matter altogether, especially when we take into account the potential *responses by third parties* to such mixed hate-love messages. Even setting aside the feelings of the targeted group (which may be legally relevant under 'hate speech' yet less so under incitement standards), audiences may get carried away by the message of hate whilst remaining deaf to the love aspect (if any). Normative statements on the very issue of sexual orientation or gender identity will very often steer close to incitement to discrimination but certainly not in all instances engage this prohibition (by comparison, incitement to violence certainly is a category of extreme speech that is more easily filtered out and flagged as a clear abuse of free speech and liable under incitement prohibitions).

For instance, a rejection of same-sex marriage may well be perceived as nothing short of an indirect denial of equality before the law, of rendering a portion of the population as second-class citizens. But for that danger to materialize, the legislator would first need to adopt the same discriminatory mindset, so the context and especially the unlikelihood of imminent discrimination defuse the speech act and may render it a contribution to the public debate on what are and are not sound laws. Similarly, a public rejection of gender identities per se will typically be tantamount to a personal denial of legal protection on that very ground.[102] But that personal denial should be distinguished from the risk of widespread denial and certainly from institutionalized denial,

---

101 *Ibid.*, para. 13, citing a Government consultation report pertaining to the Gender Recognition Act 2004.

102 See e.g. *R. (Miller) v. The College of Policing & The Chief Constable of Humberside.* Miller tweeted among other contributions to his followers: 'Transwomen are women. Anyone know where this new biological classification was first proposed and adopted?' (para. 50). In his witness statement, he held among other things, 'the potentially dangerous consequences of self-identification to existing sex based rights; the distortion of commonly understood biological concepts, such as male and female, via the introduction of enforced language, including pronouns' (para. 19).

which is not in the denier's hands, but subject to competitive politics and checks and balances.

Furthermore, the freedom of (religious) speech angle is important in this context. The extent to which statements are directed at relevant laws and policies, for example, is significant, as this would point to statements being genuine contributions to public debate. This is not to say that a rejection of same-sex marriage or of legal protection on grounds of gender identity may not engage incitement prohibitions. For instance, a public statement to the effect of challenging the (inclusive, protective) laws and policies in place accompanied by an express call to ignore the law, to breach it, to violate its norms on equal treatment and protection of reputations and dignity, and so on, could certainly engage anti-incitement standards, also when these views are religiously motivated. These considerations do not carve out a religious freedom defence. Whilst rightly emphasizing that protected religious speech could result in potentially offensive interventions in public debate and that many of these topics also *in se* have profound religious relevance, these considerations also and especially reiterate the extreme nature of punishable incitement.

Returning to the – controversial[103] – British 'saving clause', which could be seen as a direct result of the type of discussion had just now, a discussion every country dedicated to protecting free religious speech and eradicating hateful incitement is bound to have, a couple of further remarks are in order. On the one hand, such a high threshold obviously makes policing the offence a rather dire affair and considerably robs the prohibition of some of its teeth.[104] On the other hand, this type of in-built free religious speech protection is to be preferred over the previously criticized alternative of immunizing religious speech discourse through overly wide religious freedom defences. Also, the latter special guarantee pretty much decides the rights conflicts in an a priori legislative fashion, whereas the saving clause, while also a legal tool, refers the

103 The UK Government was opposed to the saving clause, but it was inserted by vote of the House of Lords (while the House of Commons was against). A notable role for the Lords Spiritual – the bishops of the established Church of England in the House of Lords – can be detected in this regard. For more legislative history and voting details, see Paul Johnson and Robert Vanderbeck, *Law, Religion and Homosexuality* (London: Routlegde, 2014), pp. 155–156.

104 Cf. Robert Wintemute, 'Homophobia and United Kingdom Law: Only a Few Gaps Left to Close?', in Luca Trappolin, Alessandro Gasparini and Robert Wintemute (eds.), *Confronting Homophobia in Europe: Social and Legal Perspectives* (Oxford: Hart, 2012), Ch.11, at p. 238 *et seq.*, calling the prohibition itself weak and fearing that the saving clause will deprive the extreme speech ban of much of its symbolic and practical value.

details of rights calibration to the judiciary. This makes for case-by-case analysis in which context factors can be taken duly into account.

The (scarce) post-2008[105] case-law appears to reflect a more robust legal assessment than did for instance the older case of *Hammond*. For example, in the first ever persecution and conviction for the offence of stirring up hatred on the grounds of sexual orientation, the Derby Crown Court dwelled on a number of pertinent content and context factors.[106] Three men were sentenced for this crime as a result of distributing leaflets on the subject of homosexuality and showing an image of an executed figure swinging from a hangman's noose. The flyers furthermore contained the following statement: 'The death sentence is the only way this immoral crime can be erased from corrupting society and act as a deterrent for any other ill person who is remotely inclined in this bent way'. While the guilty verdict was determined by a jury, Justice Burgess in his sentencing remarks reiterated a number of relevant factors. As for *content*, Justice Burgess emphasizes the extremity of the verbal attacks, especially the fact that the death sentence was contemplated by the authors of the flyers as the only appropriate measure in order to save society from some serious danger, namely from the harm of 'corruption'.[107] On the question of *intent* the jury had been satisfied that the three men had not been merely criticising homosexuality, but that their speech act had been 'threatening, and that by distributing it [they] all intended to stir up hatred against homosexuals'.[108] A number of further *context* factors are highlighted, including a sketch of the general 'background' (i.e. overall context) of the case through which the 'level of organization' behind the flyer's distribution is illustrated, the fact that the Derby gay community was specifically targeted, the 'extent' of the speech act and the intended audience ('hundreds of anti-gay leaflets were distributed' outside a mosque after Friday prayer),[109] but also a number of remarks on the issues of harm and likelihood:

> I have borne in mind that, when considering the seriousness of these offences I have to consider not only the culpability of the offender, but

105 I.e. when the amendments to relevant UK hate speech and incitement legislation were introduced.

106 Derby Crown Court, *R. v. Ihjaz Ali, Razwan Javed and Kabir Ahmed*, judgments of 20 January 2012 (conviction of three of the accused, acquitting two others) and 10 February 2012 (sentencing judgment HHJ Burgess).

107 *Ibid.* (sentencing remarks), p. 2.

108 *Ibid.*, p. 2.

109 *Ibid.*, p. 3.

> also the harm that was caused, or was intended to be caused, or might foreseeably have been caused. Here, I am obviously keen to dissuade anyone from distributing this sort of material in the future. Looking at the harm done, I have considered the threat felt by the individuals that gave evidence at the trial, and the likelihood that others were similarly affected. I have borne in mind that the residents of the streets who received this leaflet do not seem to have changed their attitude or behaviour towards their gay neighbours. Indeed it was heartening to hear one witness say that he experienced great support from his neighbours following the distribution of these leaflets. That said, you have been convicted of intending to stir up hatred. It follows that your intention was to do great harm in a peaceful community. It is also heartening that there have been no similar offences since your arrest. No-one seems to have been tempted to copy you. However, it is hard to ascertain exactly how much harm you have caused by distributing this leaflet outside the Mosque.[110]

The threshold of the domestic offence with its emphasis on 'threatening' words is considerably lower (and less objective, hence the judge's probing into the matter as to whether the hate speech victims *felt* threatened)[111] than international law's triangular incitement offence with its objective test as to whether it is likely that *third parties* will engage in harmful acts as a result of the hateful speech act. The judgment stands out for its extensive risk assessment, but also for its frankness about the ultimate difficulty as to qualifying the harms emanating from the hateful speech act. This is where socio-legal research and third-party expert input may serve an important role, akin to such amicus mechanisms at the international plane, supporting monitoring bodies and judges confronted with complex rights calibration cases by providing data that helps filling in all or various context factors.

Revisiting scripture-quoting cases in the light of a comprehensive content-intent-context test can also be revealing. For example, while charges against a Birmingham street preacher were dropped and the latter even went on to win a case against the West Midlands Police over unlawful arrest, a Dutch man who handed out flyers with scripture quotations on the subject of homosexuality was ultimately convicted. The former, Anthony Rollins, was preaching in the streets on the subject of effeminacy, quoting from the King James Bible. Someone called the police, who promptly arrested him. Judge Ashworth, for

110 *Ibid.*, p. 4.

111 See *ibid.*, p. 3: 'In the course of evidence we heard what effect, reading that leaflet had upon four homosexual men. All felt threatened'.

the Birmingham County Court, held that the circumstances of the case did not remotely engage the Public Order Act and awarded the various claims for damages.[112] Indeed, from the facts of the case – a Christian street preacher arguing that homosexual conduct is wrong; nothing more, nothing less – incitement cannot be established. Nothing in the facts points remotely to required levels of 'content', 'intent' and 'context' establishing the likelihood of imminent risk befalling the targeted group (homosexuals). The street preacher, similar in this respect to *Hammond v. DPP*, mostly managed to get himself in trouble (one bystander was reported shouting 'homophobic bigot' to the preacher),[113] although not to the extent as to raise public order issues on that front – he did not need to be 'protected against himself'. All things considered, one may discern a well-functioning marketplace of ideas in this case, where ideas are debated among members of the public and where speech meets counter-speech, albeit in this case on either side not being of the most eloquent, tolerant or politically correct type.

The contrasting Dutch case concerns a man who handed out flyers in Amsterdam containing Bible, Torah and Koran quotes on the subject of homosexuality.[114] In determining whether the offence of incitement to discrimination against homosexuals was committed, the Court of Amsterdam discusses content, intent and a number of relevant context factors. Interestingly, the fact that religious freedom is engaged here meant, the court holds, that an additional threshold test is applicable so as to determine whether the accused's behaviour is punishable. For all intends and purposes, this approach amounts to the judicial equivalent of the British saving clause. In the execution of this test, the Court, then, mobilizes a number of specific (content and intent) considerations, including the fact that the flyers also contained (false) information on correlations between homosexuality and sexual abuse of children and especially emphasized the call on 'all Muslims, Christians and Jews to unite' against the alleged harm or danger. According to the court, these factors pointed to a punishable level of *mens rea* and the need for restriction. The court's engaging with the content and intent factors can hence be deemed extensive and robust. Yet the court's engaging with the crucial likelihood question arguably leaves much to be desired. How likely was it post-flyering that imminent harm

112 Birmingham County Court, *Anthony Rollins v. West Midlands Police*, decision of 10 December 2010.

113 *Ibid.*

114 Court of Amsterdam, Case No. 13/659330-16, Judgment of 4 January 2019 (similar decisions, in separate judgments, were handed down vis-à-vis others who carried out the same act).

in the form of discriminatory or violent acts would befall the LGBT community in Amsterdam? The Amsterdam Court largely assumes this harm rather seeking to pinpoint it based on a more refined application of a context-based risk assessment. While definitive answers in the form of quantifiable harm may not be expected,[115] some context factors certainly would have yielded more exact answers here. To name but a few, the targeted audience in Amsterdam consisted of the general public, rather than a captive audience with religious preconceptions.[116] The victim target group, homosexuals in Amsterdam, also can be compared and contrasted to other contexts, notably homosexuals in non-urban areas. All such context factors help more concretely pinpointing the risk that emanated from this homophobic flyering act in Amsterdam at the material time.

5 Concluding Remarks

In conclusion, the above case-law review shows that establishing the necessity of interfering with free speech, even if hateful incitement or hate speech allegations are at stake, is a most complex judicial task. In that regard, this may be the place to point out that even *Vejdeland*,[117] whilst pivotal (see Chapter 2) in first putting protection against hate speech on the European jurisprudential map for LGBT people, was by no means the perfect precedent in terms of judicial rigour. In *Vejdeland*, both the Swedish judiciary and ultimately also the European Court of Human Rights premise the likelihood of harm on a *single* context factor: the clear tipping point for both courts is fact that the homophobic leaflets were distributed at a school, i.e. amongst young, impressionable persons.[118] The dissenting opinions in the domestic case and the separate (concurring) opinions appended to the Strasbourg Court judgment all suggest

115 Cf. Derby Crown Court in *R. v. Ihjaz Ali, Razwan Javed and Kabir Ahmed*, suggesting that we may never know the exact harm stemming from instances of hateful incitement.

116 Cf., e.g., *R. v. Ihjaz Ali, Razwan Javed and Kabir Ahmed*, concerning a more or less captive audience, viz. a Mosque.

117 European Court of Human Rights, *Vejdeland and Others v. Sweden*, Application No. 1813/07, Judgment of 9 February 2012.

118 *Vejdeland and Others v. Sweden*, para. 15 (Swedish Supreme Court: 'handing out of the leaflets took place at school') and para. 56 (European Court of Human Rights: 'young people who were at an impressionable and sensitive age'). Again, another decisive factor, for the Swedish judiciary, was the case's difference with the *Green* case in that in the latter a limited religious (sermon-setting) defence was applicable which was not available to these neo-Nazis.

that a far more robust context analysis was in order before sanctioning the incitement ('agitation') conviction. The Swedish minority judges, emphasizing the need to make 'an overall assessment of the circumstances', found a conviction not proportionate.[119] In Strasbourg, the concurring opinions make a far more comprehensive context-based risk assessment than the majority opinion does, highlighting the need for a 'careful, in-depth analysis of the aim of the speech' (i.e. intent), 'factual circumstances' (i.e. overall context), assessing 'impact' (i.e. likelihood of imminent harm on the target group), and particularly highlighting the vulnerability of the target group (LGBT people) by '[n]oting that members of the LGBT community face deeply rooted prejudices, hostility and widespread discrimination all over Europe'.[120] Furthermore, the minority shows awareness of the fact – thus connecting the factors of content, intent and the vulnerability of the target group – that attributing the spreading of sexually-transmitted diseases to homosexuals is one of the harmful stereotypes about the latter perpetuated by homophobes.[121]

It is only very recent international cases, like *Beizaras and Levickas v. Lithuania*, that show what a comprehensive judicial reasoning on matters of anti-LGBT incitement could look like.[122] Such cases, however, contain little guidance on the more specific question of calibrating specific fundamental freedoms like freedom of religious speech with the emerging state obligation to eradicate hateful homophobic and transphobic incitement. In the absence of international benchmarks, domestic (case) law shows wide varieties, offering different calibrations, ranging from more principled (legislative guarantees favouring specific principles) to more ad hoc (jurisprudential ad hoc calibrations).

While domestic legislators and especially judges have rightly put the question of resolving conflicts between free religious speech and eradicating hateful incitement on the map, and while doing justice to this complex question of colliding rights is premised on a context-based risk assessment and hence is

---

119 *Vejdeland and Others v. Sweden*, para. 16.

120 Concurring opinion of Judge Spielmann, joined by Judge Nussberger, paras. 5-6.

121 *Ibid.*, para. 6.

122 *Beizaras and Levickas v. Lithuania*, Application No. 41288/15, Judgment of 14 January 2020, which contains a very elaborate context assessment, including various references to the targeted group vulnerability (e.g. para. 79, and as frequently raised in the third-party interventions). Cf., however, another recent case: *Carl Jóhann Lilliendahl v. Iceland*, Application No. 9297/18, Judgment of 12 May 2020, being, then again, more sparse when it comes to context considerations (see paras. 45-47). See Chapter 3, especially the section on 'The Emerging ECHR Duty to Investigate Homophobic Hate Speech', for a discussion of these cases.

inevitably premised on case-by-case assessments, international human rights monitoring bodies would do well to provide more direction in the form of general comments. Specifically, *Rabat Plan of Action*-type general benchmarks on the importance of eradicating hateful incitement, on the importance of free religious speech, and on the importance of calibration through guiding principles including content, intent and context, could be consistently emphasized in the context of relevant general comments, state reporting, and in the general principles sections of international jurisprudence. Such would foster case-by-case assessment informed by context factors, promote religious freedom, while at the same time unifying the haphazard patchwork of domestic approaches to extreme speech, promote especially the anti-incitement approach, whilst dismissing overly low-threshold anti-'hate speech' approaches, and in so doing, foster legal certainty.

CHAPTER 6

Conclusion

This book has made a case for an inclusive international anti-incitement approach, thus mainstreaming existing prohibitions with the grounds of sexual orientation and gender identity, so as to protect LGBT+ persons against hateful incitement. This contribution has argued in favour of a context-based assessment of instances of hateful incitement. As far as criminal law responses to instances of hateful incitement are concerned, the content-intent-context test, as proposed by the *Rabat Plan of Action*, provides a robust legal assessment that helps put the finger on essential questions of necessity: Has the speaker truly crossed a relevant legal line (incitement) and has s/he targeted a group knowingly (intent) and was it at the material time likely that adverse acts would be committed against the targeted group (context, including the position of the speaker, the extent of the speech act, the profile of the targeted group and the likelihood of harm done to the latter).

In this legal assessment the religious nature of the speech cannot be regarded as an automatic trump, as rendering speech immune to restriction. The opposite argument has been defended within legal scholarship, for example, by Harel. This contrarian view is that 'hate speech that constitutes an integral part of a comprehensive and valuable form of life' deserves stronger protection than hate speech that is not 'deeply rooted'.[1] However, a hierarchy of speech protection does not sit well with the freedom of opinion and expression. A speech act that is not religiously motivated still engages in principle the freedom of opinion and expression. Also speech acts that are shocking/disturbing/insulting yet not at the same time religious in nature engage protection by dint of the right to freedom of opinion and expression. The fact that various human rights may overlap, freedom of religion and freedom of expression, does not mean that relevant speech acts are immune from legal scrutiny.

Again, this is not to say that the religious dimension of speech acts is not important, it is one important contextual factor that may help, within the context of alleged hateful incitement, to fill in others: audience, extent, and so on – the religious nature of the message may have a bearing on all of this and all of those factors in turn impact the key question whether or not the audience was

1 Alon Harel, 'Hate speech and Comprehensive Forms of Life', in Michael Herz and Peter Molnar (eds.), *The Content and Context of Hate Speech* (Cambridge: Cambridge University Press, 2012), pp. 306–326.

 | DOI:10.1163/9789004458864_007

incited to commit adverse act against a target group and to what extent is was likely the latter would actually occur. But it strikes as flawed to use the religious dimension to divide forms of extreme speech into categories deserving strong versus weaker protection.

Reasoning that homophobic and transphobic speech, and other hateful speech based on sexual orientation or gender identity, engage international anti-incitement law is not quite saying that each and every form of extreme speech, whether religiously motivated or not, ought to run into the penalties of criminal law. Three important points are to be made in that regard.

First, criminal law-based punishments for hateful incitement are in any event *ultima ratio*. International and regional European human rights jurisprudence[2] and authoritative interpretation agree on the point that criminal sanctions are considered the last resort when it comes to combating extreme speech. The *Rabat Plan of Action*, offering a conceptualization of Article 20(2) of the ICCPR on prohibiting hateful incitement, elaborates the point as follows:

> Criminal sanctions related to unlawful forms of expression should be seen as last resort measures to be applied only in strictly justifiable situations. Civil sanctions and remedies should also be considered, including pecuniary and non-pecuniary damages, along with the right of correction and the right of reply. Administrative sanctions and remedies should also be considered, including those identified and put in force by various professional and regulatory bodies.[3]

Second, international anti-incitement law obliges states to 'prohibit by law' hateful incitement, but penalties met out in concrete cases are in each and every case subject to the necessity and proportionality principles under the

2 *E.g.* European Court of Human Rights, *Beizaras and Levickas v. Lithuania*, Application No. 41288/15, Judgment of 14 January 2020, para. 111: 'The Court has acknowledged that criminal sanctions, including against the individuals responsible for the most serious expressions of hatred, inciting others to violence, could be invoked only as an *ultima ratio* measure'.

3 *Rabat Plan of Action on the prohibition of advocacy of national, racial or religious hatred that constitutes incitement to discrimination, hostility or violence*, Conclusions and recommendations emanating from the four regional expert workshops organised by OHCHR in 2011, adopted by experts in Rabat, Morocco on 5 October 2012 (hereafter also 'Rabat Plan'), para. 34 (endorsed by the UN OHCHR, *Report of the United Nations High Commissioner for Human Rights on the expert workshops on the prohibition of incitement to national, racial or religious hatred* (A/HRC/22/17/Add.4, 2013)). At the same time, the Rabat Plan certainly does not rule out criminal penalties ('expression that constitutes a criminal offence').

regular limitation clauses of free speech. As the Human Rights Committee puts it,

> Articles 19 and 20 are compatible with and complement each other. The acts that are addressed in article 20 are all subject to restriction pursuant to article 19, paragraph 3. As such, a limitation that is justified on the basis of article 20 must also comply with article 19, paragraph 3 ... It is only with regard to the specific forms of expression indicated in article 20 that States parties are obliged to have legal prohibitions. In every case in which the State restricts freedom of expression it is necessary to justify the prohibitions and their provisions in strict conformity with article 19.[4]

That is precisely the reason why this book has insisted on scrutinizing context factors, including especially the likelihood-of-harm notion, that foster close assessment of such 'necessity'.

Third, while hateful incitement must be 'prohibited by law', state obligations are significantly wider than merely penalizing the most heinous forms of hateful incitement. Tackling extreme speech implies a comprehensive range of measures, including preventative and other pro-active policies (known as 'positive obligations'). As the UN High Commissioner for Human Rights argued,

> it is essential to make a careful distinction between (a) forms of expression that should constitute a criminal offence; (b) forms of expression that are not criminally punishable, but may justify a civil suit; and (c) forms of expression that do not give rise to criminal or civil sanctions, but still raise concerns in terms of tolerance, civility and respect for the convictions of others.[5]

Thus, not all types of extreme speech ought to be treated equally and not all extreme speech ought to result in criminal penalties. But equally important is the consideration that state obligations in this area do not end at punishing the most extreme forms of hateful incitement. Instances that do not reach the criminal law threshold, instances that fall short of such criminal law assessment factors as likelihood and imminence, nevertheless engage state

4 Human Rights Committee, *General Comment No. 34: Article 19: Freedoms of Opinion and Expression*, CCPR/C/GC/34 (2011), paras. 50 and 52 (paragraph numbers omitted).

5 UN OHCHR, *Report of the United Nations High Commissioner for Human Rights on the expert workshops on the prohibition of incitement to national, racial or religious hatred* (A/HRC/22/17/Add.4, 2013), para. 12.

obligations. Some of these obligations may be reactive, but a significant portion of the toolkit of these positive measures that aim at the eradication of hateful incitement will be of a preventative nature. Such measures aim, among other things, at addressing prejudices, promoting diversity and tolerance, promoting equality and non-discrimination. Particularly promising recent conceptualizations of these positive measures by monitoring bodies[6] and within the literature[7] focus on promoting tolerance through education, sensitization and awareness-raising.

6 E.g., *Rabat Plan of Action*, paras. 23-29; Committee on the Elimination of Racial Discrimination, *General Recommendation 35: Combating Racist Hate Speech* (U.N. Doc. CERD/C/GC/35, 83rd session, 12-30 August 2013), paras. 30-44, listing a comprehensive set of positive measures; Special Rapporteur on Freedom of Religion or Belief, *Tackling Manifestations of Collective Religious Hatred* (A/HRC/25/58, 26 December 2013), particularly at paras. 31-53; Special Rapporteur on the Promotion and Protection of the Right to Freedom of Opinion and Expression, *Report of the Special Rapporteur to the General Assembly on Hate Speech and Incitement to Hatred* (A/67/357, 7 September 2012), particularly at paras. 56-74.

7 E.g. ARTICLE 19, *Prohibiting Incitement to Discrimination, Hostility or Violence: Policy Brief* (2012), pp. 41–45 ('Sanctions and other measures'); Peter Molnar, 'Responding to "Hate Speech" with Art, Education, and the Imminent Danger Test', in Michael Herz and Peter Molnar (eds.), *The Content and Context of Hate Speech* (Cambridge: Cambridge University Press, 2012), pp. 183–197; Maleiha Malik, 'Extreme Speech and Liberalism', in Ivan Hare and James Weinstein (eds.), *Extreme Speech and Democracy* (Oxford: Oxford University Press, 2009), pp. 96–120; David Richards, *Free Speech and the Politics of Identity* (Oxford: Oxford University Press, 1999), particularly chapters 4-6, presenting ways to promote counter-speech as a remedy; Katrine Gelber, 'Reconceptualizing Counterspeech in Hate Speech Policy', in Michael Herz and Peter Molnar (eds.), *The Content and Context of Hate Speech* (Cambridge: Cambridge University Press, 2012), pp. 198–216; Arthur Jacobson and Bernhard Schlink, 'Hate Speech and Self-Restraint', in Michael Herz and Peter Molnar (eds.), *The Content and Context of Hate Speech* (Cambridge: Cambridge University Press, 2012), pp. 217–241.

Bibliography

Bob, Clifford, 'The Global Battle over Religious Expression: Sweden's Åke Green Case in Local and Transnational Perspective', 40:2 *Journal of Ethnic and Migration Studies* (2014), pp. 212–229.

Brown, Alexander, 'The "Who?" Question in the Hate Speech Debate: Part 1: Consistency, Practical, and Formal Approaches', 29:2 *Canadian Journal of Law & Jurisprudence* (2016), pp. 275–320.

Brown, Alexander, 'The "Who?" Question in the Hate Speech Debate: Part 2: Functional and Democratic Approaches', 30:1 *Canadian Journal of Law & Jurisprudence* (2017), pp. 23–55.

Burg, Wibren van der, *Het Democratisch Perspectief: Een Verkenning van de Normatieve Grondslagen der Democratie* (Arnhem: Gouda Quint, 1991).

Callamard, Agnes, 'Religion, Terrorism and Speech in a "Post-Charlie Hebdo" World', 10 *Religion & Human Rights: An International Journal* (2015), pp. 207–228.

Cannie, Hannes, and Dirk Voorhoof, 'The Abuse Clause and Freedom of Expression in the European Human Rights Convention: An Added Value for Democracy and Human Rights Protection?', 29:1 *Netherlands Quarterly of Human Rights* (2011), pp. 54–83.

Crenshaw, Kimberlé, 'Mapping the Margins: Intersectionality, Identity Politics, and Violence against Women of Color', 46:6 *Stanford Law Review* (1991), pp. 1241–1299.

De Kerf, Justine, 'Anti-Gay Propaganda Laws: Time for the European Court of Human Rights to Overcome Her Fear of Commitment', 4:1 *DiGeSt: Journal of Diversity and Gender Studies* (2017), pp. 35–48.

Gelber, Katrine, 'Reconceptualizing Counterspeech in Hate Speech Policy', in Michael Herz and Peter Molnar (eds.), *The Content and Context of Hate Speech* (Cambridge: Cambridge University Press, 2012).

Ghanea, Nazila, 'Intersectionality and the Spectrum of Racist Hate Speech: Proposals to the UN Committee on the Elimination of Racial Discrimination', 32:4 *Human Rights Quarterly* (2013), pp. 935–954.

Harel, Alon, 'Hate speech and Comprehensive Forms of Life', in Michael Herz and Peter Molnar (eds.), *The Content and Context of Hate Speech* (Cambridge: Cambridge University Press, 2012), pp. 306–326.

Heinze, Eric, 'Cumulative Jurisprudence and Human Rights: The Example of Sexual Minorities and Hate Speech', in Phil C.W. Chan (ed.), *Protection of Sexual Minorities since Stonewall: Progress and Stalemate in Developed and Developing Countries* (London/New York: Routledge, 2010), pp. 62–78.

Irving, Alice, 'Twitter, Trans Rights and the Role of the Police: An Extended Look', UK Human rights Blog (21 February 2020, available at <https://ukhumanrightsblog.com/2020/02/21/twitter-trans-rights-and-the-role-of-the-police-an-extended-look/>).

Jacobson, Arthur, and Bernhard Schlink, 'Hate Speech and Self-Restraint', in Michael Herz and Peter Molnar (eds.), *The Content and Context of Hate Speech* (Cambridge: Cambridge University Press, 2012), pp. 217–241.

Johnson, Paul, and Robert Vanderbeck, *Law, Religion and Homosexuality* (London: Routlegde, 2014), pp. 155–156.

Keane, David, 'Attacking Hate Speech under Article 17 of the European Convention on Human Rights', 25:4 *Netherlands Quarterly of Human Rights* (2007), pp. 641–663.

Leigh, Ian, 'Hatred, Sexual Orientation Free Speech and Religious Liberty', 10 *Ecclesiastical Law Journal* (2008), at 341–344.

Leigh, Ian, 'Homophobic Speech, Equality Denial, and Religious Expression', in Hare and Weinstein (eds), *Extreme Speech and Democracy* (Oxford: Oxford University Press, 2010), p. 375.

Malik, Maleiha, 'Extreme Speech and Liberalism', in Ivan Hare and James Weinstein (eds.), *Extreme Speech and Democracy* (Oxford: Oxford University Press, 2009), pp. 96–120.

McGonagle, Tarlach, *The Council of Europe against Online Hate Speech: Conundrums and Challenges* (Council of Europe expert paper, MCM(2013)005, 2013).

Molnar, Peter, 'Responding to "Hate Speech" with Art, Education, and the Imminent Danger Test', in Michael Herz and Peter Molnar (eds.), *The Content and Context of Hate Speech: Rethinking Regulation and Responses* (Cambridge: Cambridge University Press, 2012), pp. 183–197.

Molnar, Peter, 'Responding to "Hate Speech" with Art, Education, and the Imminent Danger Test', in Michael Herz and Peter Molnar (eds.), *The Content and Context of Hate Speech* (Cambridge: Cambridge University Press, 2012), pp. 183–197.

Moon, Richard, *Putting Faith in Hate: When Religion Is the Source or Target of Hate Speech* (Cambridge University Press, 2018).

Nowak, Manfred, *U.N. Covenant on Civil and Political Rights: CCPR Commentary* (2nd rev. edn, Kehl: N.P. Engel Publishers, 2005).

Peroni, Lourdes, 'Karaahmed v. Bulgaria: The (In)Visible Racial and Religious Motivation of Violence', *Strasbourg Observers* (27 March 2015).

Plant, Richard, *The Pink Triangle: The Nazi War Against Homosexuals* (New York: Henry Holt & Company Inc, 1986).

Richards, David, *Free Speech and the Politics of Identity* (Oxford: Oxford University Press, 1999).

Stark, Sarah, 'The Expansion of Canadian Hate Speech Legislation', 10:4 *Law and Business Review of the Americas* (2007), pp. 807–118.

Stavros, Stephanos, 'A Duty to Prosecute Hate Speech under the European Convention on Human Rights?', *Oxford Human Rights Hub* (9 April 2015).

Stavros, Stephanos, 'Criminal Law Responses to Hate Speech: Towards a Systematic Approach in Strasbourg?', in Laurens Lavrysen & Natasa Mavronicola (eds.), *Coercive Human Rights Positive Duties to Mobilise the Criminal Law under the ECHR* (Oxford: Hart Publishing, 2020), pp. 117–138.

Temperman, Jeroen, 'Are State Churches Contrary to International Law?', 2:1 *Oxford Journal of Law and Religion* (2013), pp. 119–149, at pp. 121–122.

Temperman, Jeroen, 'Blasphemy and the European Court of Human Rights: A Small Step Forward, A Giant Leap Back', in Philip Czech, Lisa Heschl, Karin Lukas, Manfred Nowak and Gerd Oberleitner (eds.), *European Yearbook on Human Rights* (Cambridge: Intersentia, 2019), pp. 221–236.

Temperman, Jeroen, 'Blasphemy, Defamation of Religions & Human Rights Law', 26(4) *Netherlands Quarterly of Human Rights* (2008), pp. 517–545.

Temperman, Jeroen, 'Religious Symbols in the Public School Classroom', in Jeroen Temperman (ed.), *The Lautsi Papers: Multidisciplinary Reflections on Religious Symbols in the Public School Classroom* (Leiden/Boston: Brill/Martinus Nijhoff Publishers, 2012), pp. 143–176.

Temperman, Jeroen, *Religious Hatred and International Law: The Prohibition of Incitement to Violence or Discrimination* (Cambridge: Cambridge University Press, 2016).

Tourkochoriti, Ioanna, 'The New Regulation against Hate Speech in Greece: Strength and Weaknesses', *CritCom* (20 February 2015).

Voyles, Caroline H., and Mariana Chilton, 'Respect, Protect, and Fulfill or Reject, Neglect, and Regress? Children's Rights in the Time of the Russian "Gay Propaganda Law" ', 21:2 *Health and Human Rights Journal* (2019), pp. 325–330.

Wintemute, Robert, 'Homophobia and United Kingdom Law: Only a Few Gaps Left to Close?', in Luca Trappolin, Alessandro Gasparini and Robert Wintemute (Eds.), *Confronting Homophobia in Europe: Social and Legal Perspectives* (Oxford: Hart, 2012), Ch. 11.

www.ingramcontent.com/pod-product-compliance
Lightning Source LLC
Chambersburg PA
CBHW031329230926
51848CB00001B/155